the world of garden design

INSPIRING IDEAS FROM AROUND THE GLOBE TO YOUR BACKYARD

the world of
GARDEN
DESIGN

BY SUSAN DOOLEY

AND THE EDITORS OF *GARDEN DESIGN* MAGAZINE

THE WORLD OF GARDEN DESIGN
INSPIRING IDEAS FROM AROUND THE GLOBE TO YOUR BACKYARD

COPYRIGHT © 2000 BY
MEIGHER COMMUNICATIONS, L.P.
ALL RIGHTS RESERVED.
NO PART OF THIS BOOK MAY BE REPRODUCED
IN ANY FORM WITHOUT WRITTEN PERMISSION FROM
THE PUBLISHER.

LIBRARY OF CONGRESS CATALOGING-IN-PUBLICATION
DATA AVAILABLE.

ISBN 0-8118-2656-2

PRINTED IN HONG KONG.

DESIGNED BY
TOBY FOX, MICHAEL GROSSMAN, AND JULIE PRYMA

DISTRIBUTED IN CANADA BY
RAINCOAST BOOKS
8680 CAMBIE STREET
VANCOUVER, BRITISH COLUMBIA V6P 6M9

2 4 6 8 10 9 7 5 3 1

CHRONICLE BOOKS
85 SECOND STREET
SAN FRANCISCO, CALIFORNIA 94105

WWW.CHRONICLEBOOKS.COM

acknowledgments

As we design and plant and inevitably tear up and redo our gardens, where do our ideas come from? From around the world and around the block. *The World of Garden Design* is dedicated to tracing these ideas—back to their origins, and forward, in appropriately fresh form, into our backyards. Many members of the same merry little band of us who make GARDEN DESIGN magazine have collaborated on this book. Working from an excellent conceptual foundation laid by Douglas Brenner, the team was led by the always-wise Ann Powell. Kate Norment was a godsend as project editor; the illuminating voice of writer Susan Dooley—who gardens in Maine's zone 5—rings out on every page. The book's signature look was developed and designed by Michael Grossman, Toby Fox, and Julie Pryma, with invaluable help from Jenny Chung, Johanna Guevara, Linda Hall, Siobhan Hardy, and Amy Henderson. The photographs were researched and commissioned by Meg Matyia, María Millán, Victoria Rich, Lauren Hicks, and Amy Lundeen. Carly Hutchinson headed our crack research team, with Julia Morrill, Jennifer Matlack, Beth Chimera, and Abby Lovett; our scrupulous copy editors were Jennifer Gidman, Wendy Kagan, and Rebekkah Linton; Melissa Moss and Zoë Pellegrino wrestled our production issues with grace. For answering our call for help just when we needed it most, we are grateful to Ann McCarthy; to *GD*'s own deep throat, the omniscient Miss O; and to Julie Moir Messervy. It took Cullen Stanley, our splendid agent at Janklow & Nesbit, and at Chronicle Books, Leslie Jonath, our editor, and Julia Flagg, designer, to make this book truly happen.

This book draws on the reporting of many talented writers, notably, GARDEN DESIGN editors Carol Helms, Sarah Gray Miller, and Stephen Whitlock; and R. W. Apple Jr., Jeff Book, Jim Buckland, Miles Chapin, Ethne Clarke, James David, Page Dickey, Amy P. Goldman, Mac Griswold, Patti Hagan, Eric Hansen, Susan Heeger, Harriet Heyman, Marielle Hucliez, Madeline Hutcheson, Jamie James, judywhite, Stephen King, Leslie Li, William Bryant Logan, Steven Henry Madoff, Celia McGee, W. S. Merwin, Elizabeth Helman Minchilli, Mary Morgan, Carole Ottesen, Jean Parker Phifer, Jean Bond Rafferty, Warren Schultz, William Sertl, Mary-Sherman Willis, Holly Shimizu, Jeff Spurrier, Elaine B. Steiner, Elizabeth Stromme, Susan Allen Toth, Nora Burba Trulsson, and Stephanie Woodard. The photographers—whose work makes our pages glorious to behold—are credited on page 320. Thanks, too, to Chris Meigher, Doug Peabody, Erwin Mevorah, Mark Drucker, and Stephanie Sandberg. —*Dorothy Kalins*, Editor-in-Chief, GARDEN DESIGN

CONTENTS

A WORLD
in our backyard

Spring started slowly in the Midwest. The snow melted and the creek that ran across our land became a force that rushed and rose and overflowed its banks. It moved across the meadow and into the orchard, where for a week or so it was a muddy brown lake lapping against the tree trunks. When the waters began to recede, we were sent to clear the orchard of the flotsam left behind. Squishing through the muck, we would notice that

Italy in New Hampshire
In creating his house and garden in the artists' colony of Cornish, New Hampshire (seen here in a 1930s photograph), architect and landscape designer Charles A. Platt was inspired by the Italian gardens he had seen during his travels in 1892. His 1894 book of photographs from that trip, *Italian Gardens*, showed Americans new ways to look at formal landscapes.

the trees had begun to bloom—apples, cherries, pears—and, underneath the bridal-wreath hedge, the daffodils.

The lilacs came next, a long fragrant line we walked with our eyes closed, guided by scent instead of sight. By the time the shaggy peonies bloomed, we had shed our shoes, donned our shorts, and were running barefoot through the grass. Then school was out and the garden was moving too fast to follow. The cluster rose we called Queen Anne was covered with double pink blooms and Queen-Anne's-lace crowded the edge of the fields. Pansies, nasturtiums, marigolds, and dahlias bloomed in the intensifying heat, with fireflies lighting the evening sky, the well running dry, and grapes dangling fat and purple from the vine.

Our garden was the shape of the American summer. Or so I believed, until I grew up and discovered that the plants of my childhood were immigrants from abroad: the narcissus out of Europe, the edible cherry from England. Some had reached America on a wandering route, like the bridal-wreath, which had its beginnings in Asia; the lilac, which started in Persia; the peony, which is native to Tibet, western China, and Bhutan; the rose, which came from China; Queen-Anne's-lace, which had trekked from Eurasia; and even the native grape, which required a cross with the European *Vitis vinifera* to earn a place at the table. The American gardener has taken plants and borrowed design ideas from all over the world and—like gardeners in every place and every era—has liked nothing more than climbing into other people's beds.

The Greeks took from the Persians, the Romans from the Greeks. The French adapted the Italian style and the Dutch then copied the French. The English were influenced by the Dutch, and the Italians came full circle by uprooting their Renaissance gardens to plant English landscape parks. The Japanese borrowed from the

TIME LINE
When America
borrowed what

1500s
The birth of the backyard: Spanish, French, English, and other European colonists wall or fence their gardens to protect plants from two-legged and four-legged thieves. Native Americans don't use fences.

1500s
Melons are brought from Africa to North America, probably by the Spaniards, since English settlers find that Native Americans are already growing them.

1565–1769

The patio arrives, first in Florida, as St. Augustine is founded in 1565. Settlers at Santa Fe bring it to the Southwest in 1609. In 1769 the patio shows up in California, when Father Junipero Serra establishes the Mission San Diego de Alcalá.

1600s

English settlers embrace Native American crops but reject their planting schemes. The settlers think that corn, squash, and beans planted together in hills is too messy; they want straight furrows. Native Americans are wiser: "Three sisters"

1600s

English colonists bring in oxeye daisies as medicinal herbs, carrots to eat, and soapwort to wash clothes. They all escape the garden and run wild. We know them as white daisies (above), Queen-Anne's-lace, and bouncing bet.

1600s

Colonists import English grasses to feed cattle and make hay. By 1700 prosperous Americans are laying turf in their gardens. The great American lawn is born.

Chinese; the West so coveted the plants of the tropics that they built heated glasshouses to hold them; and in the rain forests and jungles, colonists hacked away the exuberant growth to make neat perennial borders.

With all this borrowing, you'd think that everywhere you went, gardens would look alike. Yet every garden has a soul of its own, born of what Alexander Pope called the genius of the place—and less-poetic landscape architects call the dictates of the site. Soil composed of lime or clay, beds running down a slope or planted on a plane, climate hot or climate cold—each variable means that even identical gardens put in different places will have a look of their own. There is another factor that keeps one garden from being a copy of someone else's: Our gardens are reflections of our culture and our time. Twenty years ago, who had ever heard of butterfly boxes or bat houses, much less condominiums for bumblebees? Now they are everywhere, expressing the country's concern with vanishing wildlife.

More than that, our gardens are where we plant our past, starting with the floral folklore of childhood. It takes a hard heart to ban the garden daisy, whose petals decide whether "he loves me, he loves me not," or to rid the lawn of the invasive buttercup—for what other flower, held beneath a chin, casts a soft yellow light and reveals that the chin's owner is exceedingly fond of butter?

I have consciously copied the gardens I grew up in, planting beds full to overflowing with peonies, using suckers to form a long, fragrant lilac hedge that is now, like the one of my childhood, tall enough to enclose another, secret garden. But gardens I've visited, especially those abroad, have also played a part in the way I choose and place my plants, though sometimes the borrowing is unconscious, spurred *(continued on page 17)*

1629

John Parkinson's *Paradisi in Sole* is published. It is documented in the library of Leonard Hoar, president of Harvard from 1672 to 1675. Unlike the herbals by Gerard and Culpeper, which are popular with colonists, Parkinson's book offers advice on garden design.

1637, 1642, 1654

John Tradescant the Younger travels to Virginia and brings back to England the tulip tree, the black walnut, and—surprise—poison ivy. The last would be planted in 18th-century English landscape gardens for its glossy leaves and autumn color.

1655

Tulips go from Turkey to Holland in the second half of the 16th century and are recorded as growing in New York (then New Amsterdam) by Adrian Van der Donck in 1655.

Washing...
in the Territory ...
ceded by the ...
VIRGINIA and ...
to the
United States
and by them esta...
SEAT of their G...
after the ...
MDC
Engraved by Thackara & Vallance

TOWN

POTOMAC RIVER

EASTERN BRANCH

Presidents House

Capitol

PART OF VIRGINIA WITHIN THE TERRITORY OF COLUMBIA

RYLAND WITHIN THE TERRITORY OF COLUMBIA

Perpendicular height of the West ...
... above the tide in Tiber Creek ...

...ONS
...f the

...ifices, and for the
... shapes, as they are laid
...est advantageous ground,
...ects, and the better susceptible
... or ornament may hereafter

...communication have been devised,
...distant objects with the principal,
... a reciprocity of sight at the same time
...of these leading avenues over the
...and convenience.

...ected by others running due East and
...City into Streets, Squares, &c. and these

Breadth of the S...

THE grand avenues, and such Streets as le...
places, are from 130 to 160 feet wide, and ma...
...ate foot ways, walks of trees, and a carriage...
are from 90 to 110 feet wide.

(continued from page 12) by elusive memory. Years ago, I made a garden on the roof of a Washington, D.C., brownstone. In a single hot afternoon, I carried 400 pounds of dirt, oak barrels, boards, nails, and assorted plants up four flights of stairs. The barrels held climbing roses, honeysuckle, and my cat, who thought it a perfect hiding place and thereafter confined himself to occasional indignant appearances when I forgot he lived in the honeysuckle and watered it. Two raised beds filled with tall annuals formed a barrier along the edge of the roof, so that someone dropping in would not as quickly drop out. Annual vines climbed the walls; herbs grew in containers around a small dining table. In the hazy heat of summer, I sat on a wooden bench and listened as the radios of passing cars made a single song out of a dozen disjointed melodies, and I realized I had re-created a terrace garden I'd seen wandering through Sarlat, in southwest France.

There have been other French influences—a circular parterre planted in the middle of a lawn, and a tipsy circle it turned out to be, since the land was not level. I learned from that error how geometric shapes must lie on flatter ground. Such mistakes are common on the gardener's path. It's what we do with our failures that makes our gardens unique. My circle, now planted with the fragrant Rosa 'Rose à Parfum de l'Hay'—itself an import from Paris—has become another bed, full of roses, dianthus, and malva, enlarging it and giving it a curve that changed the straight path between porch and arbor into a meandering walk among flowers.

A photograph of a garden near Grasse gave me my water garden, though it isn't edged in the brilliant tiles of heat-soaked Mediterranean countries; stone is better suited to New England, *(continued on page 20)*

Downing's Horticulturist, a Dr. Valk of Flushing, New York, describes the "Ward's Case" and reports his success with it. In the March issue, responding to a reader's query, Valk describes how to build one. Although they become fashionable furnishings in Victorian drawing rooms, the real importance of Wardian cases, as they come to be called, is that they make possible the successful transport of plants by sea from distant countries.

1830s

H. H. Hunnewell visits England and comes home to Wellesley, Massachusetts, to create the first Italian garden in the United States, inspired by a British version.

1830s

Thomas Drummond discovers annual phlox in Texas and sends seeds to Glasgow, where more vividly colored cultivars are developed. These return to America a few years later and become garden favorites: just one example of an American wildflower that other nations have bred into worthy garden plants and returned to us. Others include New England and New York asters, monarda, and, most recently, lisianthus.

mid-1800s

British inventions like J. C. Loudon's wrought-iron glazing bar, which could be bent and curved—and used in building domed, all-glass greenhouses like the Palm House at Bicton—are reported in U.S. horticultural magazines and gradually adopted by Americans. The palm house in San Francisco's Golden Gate Park (above) was completed in 1879.

mid-1800s

Bedding out—moving colorful annuals from greenhouse to garden to create patterns—is brought to America by travelers to Europe. One popular bedding flower, the petunia, bred from species found in Argentina and Uruguay, arrives from Scotland at the same time.

1849-82

During his postings in Turkey and Italy, American diplomat George Perkins Marsh studies the consequences of deforestation in the Middle East and along the Mediterranean. His *Man and Nature: Physical Geography as Modified by Human Action*, first published in 1864, points out that protecting forests can prevent droughts, floods, and disastrous climate changes.

(continued from page 17) where I live. But it does have water lilies and a solar-powered fountain, which sends a gentle spray down on six waiting frogs.

The French also inspired me to change my original raised vegetable beds into a more ornamental potager, though that is too proper a name for a place that always needs weeding. In taking that French idea, I should also have taken their meticulous care (or at least a gardener), but work and weather have always stepped on my best intentions. Still, there are grapevines growing on a wooden fence, a peach tree in the precise center of the plot, and paths dividing rectangular beds, which hold a mixture of herbs, vegetables, and flowers. The lettuce is planted in colorful blocks: 'Red Sails' set among pale green 'Buttercrunch' and purple orach standing sentinel in back. Though I had wanted to plant espaliered apples along one side—an idea I saw in Kent— my climate is too harsh and that spot too wet. So, I planted a permanent structure instead: a line of terra-cotta chimney pots, each three feet high, holding billows of white cosmos.

There are strawberry beds edged in borage, whose leaves are an essential garnish in that traditional English drink, Pimm's Cup. There is sorrel, because once having tasted sorrel soup in a Paris bistro, I had to grow my own. There are beans growing on poles, just as they have done for centuries in the cottage gardens of England, and there are tomatoes from South America. These are also meant to grow on poles, but invariably they shimmy on down to the ground. There are nasturtiums from Peru, marigolds and morning glories from Mexico. There is calendula, a plant that originated in India and has long been used to make a healing salve. Because of my six Shetland sheep, who wait for weeds on the far side of the fence, *(continued on page 24)*

1850

Andrew Jackson Downing visits England for the first time. He comes home convinced of the superiority of American trees and shrubs: "We had always excused ourselves . . . for the well known neglect of the riches of our native Flora, by saying that what we can see any day in the woods is not the thing by which to make a garden distinguished. . . . But, indeed, one has only to go to England, where 'American plants' are the fashion . . . to learn that he knows very little about [their] beauty."

1850

On his walking tour of England and the Continent, Frederick Law Olmsted is impressed by Joseph Paxton's Birkenhead Park in Liverpool. Its design will influence his thinking when he and Calvert Vaux plan New York City's Central Park in 1858.

1892
Florence Boit visits France and learns to play golf. On her return, she has the first private golf course in New England constructed on one of her family's estates.

1892
Charles A. Platt and his brother travel to Italy. Platt publishes the photographs he took on the trip in *Italian Gardens* in 1894.

1904
Edith Wharton publishes *Italian Villas and Their Gardens*, with illustrations by Maxfield Parrish (above). Platt's and Wharton's books set off a craze for Italian gardens in this country.

23

(continued from page 20) there are Fuller's teasels, plants of eight or nine feet that stand on the edges of the herb bed like the columns of an ancient ruin. I grow them out of curiosity, having seen them in a neglected Suffolk field. All of this goes on, in vegetable plots and orchards and beds full of perennials, because my garden isn't just for food and flowers. It's for geography and history and mystery. I have mapped the English countryside with the hundreds of daffodils planted on the banks of my pond, and a hedgerow of elder and roses that shields a meadow from the road. Last summer, when rain never fell and the sun became a guest who wouldn't go, it came to me that my garden lacked the cool greens of Italy. Maine is too cold for the dark cypress to survive, but come spring I will plant more arborvitae to give my garden green bones.

A garden's geography lies not just in the styles it borrows from other places but in the plants as well. When a lust for tulips makes me empty my pockets for bulbs, I feel a kinship with the Ottoman Turks, who had a mania for the flower—in the 16th century, Sultan Selim II ordered 350,000 of them. My passion for peonies makes me visualize a 14th-century Chinese scholar, taking up a brush to make a delicate rendition of a favored bloom. I know the Roman soil where the poet Virgil walked, because, like him, I have learned the value of manuring the land and of letting it lie fallow: "But sweet vicissitudes of rest and toil / Make easy labour, and renew the soil. / Yet sprinkle sordid ashes all around, / And load with fattening dung thy fallow ground."

There is both geography and history in the story of two gardeners touring English estates at the end of the 18th century. Thomas Jefferson and John Adams were men who loved the soil, and they occasionally shared jaunts into the English countryside. Jefferson was excited by all he saw, making copious notes that would later

Plant hunter David Fairchild helps
arrange a gift of 2,000 flowering
cherry trees from the mayor of
Tokyo to be planted along the Tidal
Basin in Washington, D.C. Much
embarrassment ensues when the
first shipment is destroyed because

inspectors in Seattle find it to be
diseased. A new gift of healthy
trees is finally planted.

Fletcher Steele collects ideas from
European gardens on annual trips
and orchestrates them to suit
himself and his clients. He adapts
a French parterre for the floor of
the Afternoon Garden at Naumkeag in Massachusetts. Its columns
are a whimsical mixture of Nor-

wegian, Venetian, and medieval
inspiration. Later, in writing about
the Chinese Garden designed after
he and Naumkeag's owner visit
China, he describes the estate as "a
Traveler's garden, bringing home to
America the best of foreign life and
habits to enrich our ways here."

1928

The Garden Club of America endows a fellowship in landscape architecture at the American Academy in Rome.

1945

James Rose is first exposed to Japanese culture in Okinawa during World War II military service. He uses shoji panels—made of translucent plastic rather than rice paper—as screening for a small city garden in 1950. In subsequent visits

to Japan he finds much to learn, but he makes very clear in his 1965 book *Gardens Make Me Laugh* that he doesn't believe in trying to make Japanese gardens in the U.S. (His home in Ridgewood, New Jersey, is shown above. You decide.)

1960s

Mrs. Edgar Stern and her architect, William Platt, go to Spain. When they come back, they remake the south lawn of Longue Vue, her Shipman-designed garden in New Orleans, adding a water channel inspired by the Alhambra.

find fulfillment in his gardens at Monticello. But though Jefferson is my garden hero, it was Adams who won my heart. He, too, made notes, though they were terser, more dour, finding as much to reject as to admire. Seeing a series of dung heaps lined up on the edge of a pasture, each heap treated a little differently, this farmer-patriot concluded: "This may be good manure, but is not equal to mine, which I composed in heaps on my own farm, of horse dung from Bracketts stable in Boston, marsh mud from the sea shore and street dust from the plain at the foot of Pens Hill in which is a mixture of marl." Others may find Adams in his letters and speeches. I am happier by far to find him in my compost heap.

There is a worn-out image of the gardener bent over the weedy bed—a stodgy, homebound soul, never crossing any border but the perennial one along the lawn. But we also know the gardener as an adventurer, traveling through space and time, planting geography and harvesting history, aware of the mystery of nature, taking things we've seen in a world full of gardens and miraculously making them our own. To give this modern-day gardener fresh ideas, *The World of Garden Design* looks hard at regions that have had the greatest influence on the way our gardens grow. Each chapter begins with the design themes—those instantly identifiable stylistic elements—that shape a country's garden legacy: the parterre in France, the terraced gardens of Italy, England's perennial borders, Japan's Zen gardens, and both the lush growth of the rain forest and the sparse beauty of the desert. After we explore these historic and stylistic precedents, we turn to "Bringing It Home" and "Garden Tour," robust sections where we show how foreign influences have been freely and imaginatively interpreted on American soil. May these garden travels inspire you to behold, borrow, and create.

1975

Seed Savers Exchange is founded in Decorah, Iowa, to conserve and promote heirloom vegetables, fruits, and flowers through a grassroots network of 8,000 seed collectors. Their collection of some 18,000 varieties holds seeds from every corner of the world, including seeds believed to have been brought to America on the *Mayflower*.

1988

Texan John Croslin's neighbor brings back a *homi* as a souvenir from Korea. Croslin is so taken with the versatility and stylishness of the traditional garden tool that he imports it. It is sold here as the EZ-Digger, Asian Hand Plow, or Ho-mi Cultivator.

ITALY
and the mediterranean

- THE OUTDOOR ENCLOSURE

- SCULPTING IN STONE

- PLAYING WITH WATER

- CONTAINER PLANTING

The soft golden stone of a villa hugging the hillside, a flanking guard of cypress trees, grapevines stretching across a field in the flickering dance of sunshine and shadow: It could be a photograph taken yesterday in the Tuscan countryside. It could be a picture painted in the 15th century for Cosimo de' Medici. ■ For more than two thousand years, the terrain and the climate of Italy have dictated the shape of its gardens, setting them on terraces carved out of rugged hillsides, cooling them with the spray of falling water, shading them from the harsh summer sun with the dark sentinel cypress and the light green leaves of ilex. ■ Rome may have been the imperial city, but its young men dreamed of the *villa rustica*, where they could retreat into the world of vineyards and olive groves and watch golden carp swim in their shallow pools. The poet Horace declared himself content with "a piece of ground not over large; with a garden, and near to the house a stream of constant water." ■ The Goth invasions destroyed the gardens of the Roman Empire, and neither Visigoths nor Ostrogoths raging through the classical villas and encountering menageries carved from boxwood showed any inclination to exchange their spears for shears. As they did in the rest of Europe, during the years of war and invasion, the gardens of the Mediterranean grew near the house. But inside the *hortus conclusus*, the "enclosed garden," the memory of other gardens lived on: the lushly planted, water-filled *pairidaeza* of the Near East, first brought to the West by Xenophon on his return from Persia; the gardens of ancient Rome, which stepped out of the villa like rooms without roofs. ■ In the 15th century, with the countryside once again secure, Italians read the rural rhapsodies of Roman poets and studied the city's marble ruins, then they built their villas on hillsides overlooking the spectacular countryside and surrounded them with gardens that, while borrowing from

A TERRA-COTTA SPHINX (ABOVE) WATCHES OVER 8,000 ROSE SPECIES AND HYBRIDS AT ROSETO BOTANICO DI CAVRIGLIA CARLA FINESCHI. OPPOSITE: THE GARDENS OF IMPERIAL ROME DREW ON ANCIENT EGYPTIAN MODELS, WHOSE ENCLOSING WALLS, CENTRAL POOLS, AND SHADE TREES WERE DEPICTED IN DETAILED TOMB PAINTINGS. PRECEDING PAGE: THE GARDEN OF THE HOTEL SANTA CATERINA IN AMALFI OCCUPIES A TERRACED HILLSIDE OVERLOOKING THE SEA.

the past, created something new. ■ It was the great gift of the Italian gardener to se the natural advantages of his incomparable landscape, and to fit them into his schem with an art which concealed itself," wrote Edith Wharton in her classic *Italian Villas an Their Gardens*. ■ The blistering heat of Italian summers made flowers, in Wharton words, a "parenthetical grace," grown in containers or in the *giardino segreto* adjacent to the house. The style of the Renaissance gardens was in the green of trees, in the coo ness of water, and in structures made of stone: terraces linked by curving steps, column twined with vines, loggias and grottoes to provide shade from the sun. "The inherer beauty of the garden lies in the grouping of its parts—in the converging lines of its long ilex-walks, the alternation of sunny open spaces with cool woodland shade the proportion between terrace and bowling-green, or between the height of a wa and the width of a path," Wharton wrote. ■ Proportion was everything—paths wid enough for people to walk abreast, columns built to a thickness one-tenth of the length, loggias designed to shield from the summer sun while still catching the angula rays of winter. ■ Wharton warned that "a marble sarcophagus and a dozen twiste columns will not make an Italian garden." It is the ideas: that the architecture of garden must be in keeping with the style of the house, that there should be transitiona planting so that the formal garden does not stumble up against the untamed country side, and that a garden must be suited not only to its site and its climate but also to th needs of its owner. During the Renaissance, that meant places to walk and discuss ph losophy while surrounded by the splash of a fountain and the sweet scent of lemon. I our time, it may mean an easily tended garden whose beauty comes from perfect pro portions, the subtle use of stone, the shade of trees, and the soothing sound of wate

elements of **italian** garden style

giardino segreto A "secret garden." During the Renaissance the *giardino segreto* was adjacent to the house and was the part of the garden where most flowers were grown, among them violets, roses, lilies, and lavender.

loggia Like the pergola and the arbor, the loggia may support vines, but its purpose is to protect not plants but people. It is a roofed gallery or arcade that provides shade from the summer sun and is used for strolling, with one or more of its sides open to the air.

pergola An arbor formed of plants trained over trelliswork, a pergola can be a freestanding covered walk or can be attached to the side of a building. Although it offers a shady spot in the garden, its primary function is to support vines. In formal gardens, the pergola usually consists of stone or marble columns holding wooden cross beams overhead.

balustrade Lovers in novels always wander out onto the terrace and lean against the balustrade, a series of short pillars or columns topped with a rail or coping.

column In classical architecture, the slender shaft commonly called a column was only part of the whole. The shaft rested on a base and was topped by a capital, which generally supported a railing or the decorative part of a building. Sometimes the shaft took the form of a caryatid, a standing female figure.

sala scoverta An enclosed courtyard or uncovered room that opened from the house and was treated in a similar style. The climate of the Mediterranean made the distinction between rooms with roofs and rooms without of much less importance than it was in the north.

colonnade A series of columns set at regular intervals and usually supporting the base of a roof structure. Italian Renaissance gardens often incorporated such classical architectural elements.

grotto Sometimes an actual cave or cavern, a grotto is generally a man-made retreat from the sun's heat. Often set into the courtyard walls of Italian villas, grottoes are cool, damp places where classical sculptures (as at the Villa La Pietra, opposite) might reside.

the outdoor enclosure

The walls whisper with the soft buzz of insects, shiver when the wind rises up. Should someone stumble against them, they spread apart and receive the clumsy visitor in a green embrace. These trees and bushes, clipped to a single, dense plane, form intimate rooms in the larger garden and are as much a barrier as the courtyard walls of stone.

In the Mediterranean, people wander easily between rooms with a roof and those without—*sala scoverta*, they call them, or "uncovered rooms," as though the house had meandered on, leaving the roof behind. If a villa has rooms, a garden should, too: Flowers are grown in a *giardino segreto*, or "secret garden." When the blooms falter in the summer heat, one moves to another room, where a loggia provides shade, a fountain cools the air, and a dark grotto offers a damp retreat from the sun.

In the 19th century the *giardino inglese* became all the rage—misty, romantic English landscapes stretching as far as the eye could see. They were northern gardens, unsuited to rocky hills and glaring sun, but fashion is often folly, and the green rooms were chopped to the ground.

In the 20th century owners of many of those same villas ferreted out the classical plans, mended terraces and courtyard walls, and replanted the trees and shrubs that formed the green rooms. Such reinstatement must have been sweet revenge for the ghost of the Renaissance gardener, but there was more. It is common today in the *giardino inglese* to find room after room, this one planted with spring bulbs, that one with all white flowers. The occupants linger in each for its time of bloom and then, in practical, Mediterranean style, they slam the door behind them.

WALLS OF GREEN
The Italian garden, as illustrated in the 1839 book *The Flower Garden* (above). Opposite: One green room leads to another in the restored gardens of La Pietra in Tuscany. In the foreground, clipped boxwood and yews surround a central fountain, watched over by a line of ancient statues. In the next sala scoverta, a vine-covered loggia provides shade from the Tuscan sun.

FRAMING SPACE

In classic Italian style, low boxwood hedges frame potted lemon trees at the Villa La Foce (this page). The multilevel terraced garden, which overlooks Tuscany's Orcia valley, was designed in the 1920s and '30s as a fresh interpretation of Renaissance formality. Opposite: The pilastered courtyard of the Villa Aurelia, home of the American Academy in Rome, serves as a backdrop for a fountain sculpture by Paul Manship, which was installed in 1921. Jasmine climbs the pilasters, and the courtyard is shaded by cypress. The grounds of the 17th-century villa were recently restored by a team headed by American landscape architect Laurie Olin.

39

sculpting in stone

The Mediterranean gardener, who lives with a rocky soil, long ago learned to make an obstacle into art. Stone, from the crudest volcanic tufa to the finest marble, has been sculpted into columns, hollowed into basins, and chiseled into the features of a perfect god.

There are stone arches, pillars, and urns, and stone steps leading up to another level of stone. It wasn't just raw rocks turned up in a field or marble freshly cut from a quarry. There were the sculpted gods of the empire's past scattered around in the ruins. Renaissance architects, studying Hadrian's villa, often left with a statue or two.

The Mediterranean farmer must have felt both deviled and delighted by stone. Although it was there to use, it was also always *there*. But farmers everywhere know how to use what the earth has to offer, and in the Mediterranean the rocks that obstructed the crop were unearthed to make hillside houses and terraced fields of olives and grapes.

In the Renaissance gardens, gods of stone stand on pedestals set into stone niches; goddesses, their draperies falling in marble folds, line up on a terrace wall. Mythological beasts lurk in grottoes. Neptune conquers the sea, or at least a massive fountain, and in one green room after another, statues gleam white against a background of verdant boxwood. The statues of the Mediterranean garden are a constant presence, sliding by almost unseen or appearing suddenly as you turn a corner, as emphatic as an exclamation point at the end of a sentence.

The secret hidden in the stone is that a garden not only needs a general shape; it needs surprising details to draw the eye.

LIVING HISTORY
In the gardens of Tuscany, history is carved in the stone. A deity (above) surveys one of the gardens at the Villa La Foce near Pienza. Opposite: The ochre stone of Venzano, a former monastery whose owners raise aromatic plants, is repeated in the borders of the raised beds, which hold a collection of old-fashioned dianthus.

SHELTERING STONE

At the Parco Giardino Sigurtà (this page), which occupies the grounds of an abandoned 17th-century villa near Verona, a small stone bench overgrown with vines is both decorative and functional. Opposite: Stone serves as structure and focal point in the gardens at Ninfa, created in the crumbling ruins of a medieval town near Rome. Here a small statue nestles into a niche in an ancient castle wall.

playing with water

Water is renewal. Without it, plants and people die. It cleans the body and soothes the soul. And if it would come only when it was wanted, the world would be a green and glorious place. But it doesn't, and from earliest times people have devised ways to regulate it—dikes to hold back floods and ditches to send rivers into drought-parched fields.

As early as 2200 B.C., Assyrians were using a *shaduf,* a long pole with a bucket on one end and a counterweight on the other, to draw water—as much as 600 gallons a day—from a river or well. Aqueducts were in use in Greece from the sixth century B.C., but it was the pump, invented in the third century B.C. by Ctesibius of Alexandria, that turned a trickle into a flood.

The Romans used water to spectacular effect—piping it through aqueducts all over the empire, constructing baths and letting fountains flow—until the fifth century A.D., when repeated hostile incursions pulled the plug. When the Arabs drove the Goths out of Spain in the eighth century, they brought with them much of the knowledge that had been lost to the West in the intervening years. They irrigated the arid countryside, making gardens wherever they went, like the spectacular water gardens of Alhambra and the Generalife in Granada.

The Renaissance gardeners of Italy, taking inspiration from the Moors, produced the wonders of Tivoli, where water tumbled down staircases, fell from fountains, gushed, sprayed, and flowed with a constant murmuring. Like the sound of birds and the wind rustling through grass, the splash of water is part of the Mediterranean garden's song.

WATERWORKS
The Renaissance delight in water reached its culmination at the Villa d'Este in Tivoli. The Line of a Hundred Fountains (detail above) carried three channels of water, representing the rivers that connect Tivoli and Rome. Opposite: An underground chamber concealed within the Fountain of the Organ created hydraulic pressure that opened and closed organ pipes, playing five tunes.

NINFA NATURALISM

At Ninfa, near Rome, the Caetani family created a romantic garden that combines the natural beauty of the site with plants collected from all over the world. Gelasio Caetani laid out a series of canals in the 1920s to divert water from the river running through the property. In 1976 the Italian government set aside close to 5,000 acres around Ninfa as a nature sanctuary, and the grounds are now open to the public.

EARTHLY PARADISE
The Alhambra and the Generalife, begun in the 13th century, were meant to serve as a terrestrial paradise for the ruling Nasrid dynasty of Granada, Spain. As in other Moorish palaces, water was used both to cool the gardens and courtyards and to create a contemplative oasis. A long central pool at the Generalife (this page) is bordered by box-wood hedges and cypress. Opposite: The fountain in the Alhambra's Patio de los Leones rests on 12 marble lions spouting water.

container planting

Everyone wants what someone else has. Take lemons, for instance. Introduced by the Arabs into Spain in the 12th and 13th centuries, the tree with its pale green leaves and sweet-scented flowers spread throughout the Mediterranean. Everyone wanted a lemon tree, even in regions where winter temperatures dropped below freezing and the fruit could not survive. Gardeners then did what gardeners do now: They planted the trees in pots and, in the winter, moved them to the *stanzone,* or "lemon house," to keep them from the cold.

The pot, a microregion where both soil and climate can be controlled, lets the gardener play god and grow plants that won't survive in the ground. With this power comes the responsibility to provide the rain, the sun, and the shade. When Greek women in the fifth century B.C. celebrated the festival of Adonis, they planted seeds in earthenware pots and left them on rooftops where, in the midsummer heat, they quickly germinated, withered, and died. This was done not because the women were careless gardeners, but because they wanted to honor Adonis, who died young.

To Mediterranean gardeners, pots were not only practical but also beautiful, not just ordinary clay but the pink terra-cotta of Impruneta in Tuscany, favored since Etruscan times. Although a pot may be filled with flowering plants to add color to a courtyard or a garden room, just as often it is given prominence because of its shape—a classical urn on a pedestal, a line of bulbous pots set on a balustrade. A pot is not just a container to hold a plant; it's an object made to admire.

POTS ON THE PATH
A terra-cotta urn (above) occupies a niche along the drive leading to the Villa Aurelia in Rome. Opposite: At Venzano in Tuscany, a sculpted head peers out of a stone wall with lavender above, while dianthus, *Iris pallida*, and *Salvia officinalis* spill out of stone-edged beds punctuated by pots holding gazania and *Tanacetum densum*.

POTTED ACCENTS
A procession of potted lemon trees on the lawn at the Villa Massei (this page) in Tuscany reinforces the boundaries of an outdoor room formed by cypresses and palms. Traditionally, lemon trees were stored in specially designed structures for protection from the winter cold. Opposite: Potted trees flank a portal at the Villa Aurelia, while spiky accents in terra-cotta urns call attention to the balustrade above.

53

bringing it
HOME

The dictum that the garden must relate to the house, and that both must be at home in the landscape, has made many Americans feel barred from the Italian garden. As for having Venus lurking in the laurels, we may feel foolish dotting our gardens with the materials and gods of another place and time. What we can take from the Mediterranean is the magic that Edith Wharton, who created her own Italian garden in Massachusetts, described as "the blending of different elements, the subtle transition from the fixed and formal lines of art to the shifting and irregular lines of nature, and...the essential convenience and livableness of the garden." Instead of a classical balustrade on a terraced hillside, a Pennsylvania gardener uses a whimsical one of wood to keep the geese from the garlic; instead of a formal marble fountain, a designer in Washington, D.C., creates a spray of water gushing from a granite walk. As gardens move from place to place, they change as much as we do.

ENCLOSURE: SECRET GARDEN

Relating to Her Surroundings

Like a Mediterranean gardener, Denise Woolery views her Santa Barbara, California, garden as both an extension of the house and a response to the environment. When she repainted the house in an ocher color reminiscent of Tuscan farmhouses, she was inspired to add new plants in complementary colors, like the climbing rose 'Angel Face', which has deep mauve blooms. Designing her garden with what she calls "an eye for the natural landscape," Woolery has intermingled tough, drought-tolerant yarrow with lavender, bird-of-paradise, and California native sage. An *Acacia boormanii* by the corner of the house is underplanted with bulbinella, and an apple tree stands among daylilies and scented-leaved geraniums.

55

Pool of Tranquillity

Landscape architect Judy Murphy set her Lakeville, Connecticut, pool firmly in the Mediterranean tradition. To avoid a tall and unattractive fence (often required by law), she created her enclosed garden room by placing it in a courtyard formed by the side of a barn, a lilac hedge, and a pergola holding grapevines. The final side of the room was made by erecting a 9-foot-high stone wall (right) and flanking it with pergolas backed with wire mesh, hidden by the growth of Virginia creeper. As a final classical touch, Murphy put cast-iron columns (left) at the edge of the pool.

ENCLOSURE: PATHWAY

From the Casual . . .

A hillside (left) becomes a separate room in the hands of Los Angeles designer Chris Rosmini, who felt a Mediterranean-style garden would best suit her Mediterranean-style house. Using leftover bricks from her landscaping jobs and scavenged chunks of broken concrete, she has constructed walks, walls, and stairs to provide a structural framework for her plants. Drought-tolerant artemisia, *Salvia canariensis*, *Plectostachys serphyllifolia*, and lavatera grow on the hillside, while dwarf pampas grass thrives in a pot.

. . . to the Formal

At Filoli (right), near Woodside, California, visitors move from one enclosed garden to the next, each with its own distinct character. The most dramatic room is a long, narrow allée of Irish yews, bordered with candytuft and potted daffodils. The gardens of Filoli, which was built at the turn of the century as the country estate of gold-mine heir William Bourn, were designed by Bruce Porter. Filoli is now open to the public.

At the Deep End

An enclosed courtyard garden (left) in upstate New York is the imaginative creation of Jessica Williams, who converted her family's abandoned swimming pool into a private garden room. What she calls "the pool's peculiar ecosystem"—a sloping surface and poor drainage—forced her to plant drought-tolerant plants like artemisia and lavender in the shallow end, leaving the deep end for moisture-loving astilbes and hostas.

On the Far Side

One of the garden rooms (right) created by George A. "Frolic" Weymouth at his estate in Pennsylvania's Brandywine River valley is defined by an old iron gate and walls of hollyhocks and living hornbeams. Like other areas in the estate's gardens, the "house," haunted by sculptor Rob Jones's *Ghost* (in the doorway at the far end), helps create a sense of occasion.

Party Room

Landscape designer Jon Carloftis designed a garden room (left) "for clients who like to party." The Bucks County, Pennsylvania, site had 8-foot-high fieldstone walls, the remnants of a 19th-century barn. Carloftis paved the room with fieldstone, planted a narrow border that would leave the room's 25-by-50-foot space intact, and added a fountain for water lilies and wild flag irises. To make an entrance, he built an arched pergola and covered it with vines. "We should put as much thought into outdoor spaces as we do into interior ones," says Carloftis.

Growing Room

In another Bucks County garden, Renny Reynolds and Jack Staub have taken a Mediterranean idea and made it as American as apple pie, dotting the grounds of their Boxwood Farm not with formal garden rooms but with "vegetable garden" rooms. One room (right) is surrounded by a jigsaw filigree fence, which Reynolds recycled from a display he designed for a garden show.

Do-It-Yourself Classicism

Gardening is about space, says Bennett Bean, master ceramicist and creative gardener. "First you understand space," he says, "then you put structures in it. Only *then* should you plant trees, shrubs, and finally, flowers." Applying an artist's eye to the landscape, Bean has designed columns, colonnades, and installations to place throughout the rolling farmland of his 10-acre domain in western New Jersey. The extruded terra-cotta columns of his classic pergola (left), now softened by grapevines and roses, were created with a machine he designed himself. A limestone table next to the pergola holds a porcelain bowl from Bean's *Running Man* series.

65

Diana and Rose

On the Long Island estate of garden writer C. Z. Guest, an 18th-century French bronze statue of the goddess Diana (left) is framed by borders of hybrid tea, grandiflora, and floribunda roses. Offsetting the classical formality is a casual Guest gesture: giving the huntress her own rose to hold. The statue presides over one of three outdoor rooms Guest has created close to the house and en- closed with yew hedges.

Classical Kitsch

Fashion designer Betsey Johnson makes up-to-the- second clothes with hot color and great flair. And she's done the same with her garden (right), located on a penthouse terrace 18 stories above Greenwich Village in New York City. The deck and the trellis are lavender and the pots yellow. An ersatz sheep wanders among imitation roses that bloom near a real hydrangea. Even Johnson's version of classical sculpture shows her sense of humor.

STONE: TERRACE

Recycling the Renaissance

Like the Renaissance garden designers, landscape architect Michael Van Valkenburgh of Cambridge, Massachusetts, believes that the framework of a garden should be visually satisfying. He also shares their belief that "human needs, not just those of the artist or designer, help to mold what is designed." When he created a sculpted garden for clients on Martha's Vineyard, he reinterpreted the classical elements of marble columns and stone terracing in an updated, minimalist design. The crisp, curved walls of recycled granite not only tame the irregular site but also relate the garden to the house and both to the landscape. The lighthouse, a local landmark, is visible from every area of both porch and garden.

Playing Pool

Scott Johnson, an architectural and landscape designer, used his own Bridgehampton, New York, house to create a fantasy in stone and water. His two-room pool house rises out of the water, with the cellar windows only inches from the pool's surface. "It's meant to be fun," Johnson says of his backyard moat. Stones that were hand-set into gunite (right) imitate the easy entry of a sloping beach before the pool begins to drop, reaching 11 feet beneath the balcony. Johnson used a wide array of stone for his poolside folly—Nevada quartzite for the house, flagstone for the front patio, river rock and Japanese garden stones for the beach entry, and granite boulders for the edging. The carved pink sandstone windowsill beneath the balcony (left) was salvaged from a Washington, D.C., brownstone.

Out to Sea

When wildfires burned the Malibu, California, home of Jeannette and Kenneth Chiate, only the swimming pool survived. Seen on its own, the pool seemed to lead directly to the sea. Impressed with their new open view, the Chiates asked landscape architect Pamela Burton to pull together the pool, the sea, and the sky. The pool's solid cliffside border was replaced with an infinity edge, over which water appears to flow out to sea (though it actually spills into a hidden catch basin and is recycled). And instead of traditional plantings, Burton added euphorbia and agave, which grow from pockets in a patio that is low enough not to block the expansive ocean views.

73

Water Rising

A modest three-foot geyser (left) rises from granite blocks set in a garden path. Designers Yunghi Choi Epstein and Joanne Lawson sited the fountain so that it formed a "seamless part of the path" (bottom right), and the water disappears with the flick of a switch. For the mechanics of the fountain (top right), a small underground reservoir made of poured concrete was equipped with a recirculating pump. Water shoots out between the stones, which rest on a metal grate. The pump is connected to an upright copper pipe; a flow valve, installed by a plumber, controls the height of the jet. An electrician hard-wired the pump directly to the house, burying the cable deep in the ground and installing an electrical switch at the back door.

Simpler to install than a concrete basin, a plastic tub (1) works fine. Paired flowerpots stacked mouth to mouth and filled with lava rock (2) act as a filter for the submersible pump (3). The water surge is adjusted by the pipe's flow valve (4). Landscape cloth or polyethylene sheets (5) reduce weeds and debris. A sturdy metal grate (6) keeps water clean and kids safe; it's easily camouflaged by stones (7).

Pot Luck

When a handmade pot (left) that landscape architect James David had ordered from Italy arrived broken in two, he made the best of it. After making the broken edges even with a masonry saw, he mortared the pot to the limestone wall of his Austin, Texas, garden, then filled it with a prickly pear cactus native to Mexico.

Paradise Contained

The 300-square-foot garden of Allison Fonte is in the middle of New York City, on a roof four flights above the street. By combining a tent right out of the Arabian Nights for privacy, a fountain filled with Japanese jade stones for water music, and an array of plants in pots for greenery, Fonte has created her own Mediterranean *pairidaeza*. Airy bamboo and *Miscanthus sinensis* create a screen without blocking light, and a peegee hydrangea rises above pots of herbs and variegated ivy. "With container gardening," says Fonte, "you can move plants around as they grow and change."

CONTAINERS: ORNAMENT

Tuscan Terra-Cotta

The clay of Impruneta in Tuscany, once used by 15th-century sculptor Luca Della Robbia, is still prized for its pink and earthy tones. Artisans spend up to a month turning out a single piece. Because the terra-cotta is fired for an entire week at 2,000°, the finished pots are tough enough to stay outside through frosty winters. The collection of pots at left, imported by Seibert & Rice in Short Hills, New Jersey, were planted with delphinium, acanthus, rudbeckia, lobelia, and lantana by Rebecca Cole, a garden designer and garden shop owner in New York City.

Pots with a Past

Garden ornaments (such as these, right) are designed to withstand the extremes of wind and weather, and it doesn't matter if they show their age. For objects in the garden, a little distress is a good thing. Designed to hold plants, both the 19th-century limestone urn (top) and the pair of turn-of-the-century terra-cotta urns (bottom) can have a practical purpose or be used to draw the eye to the end of a garden path.

Trendy Terra-Cotta

The tradition of planting in pots is updated in terra-cotta planters (top left) and architectural pottery from the 1950s (bottom left). These contemporary containers are among the details in the garden of Kathy Guild, who is co-owner of Outside, a Los Angeles store that specializes in mid-century modern patio furniture. The seamless integration of indoors and outdoors in the modernist houses of Southern California inspired a liberal reinterpretation of the Italian garden room.

Heavy-Duty Pots

Hand-turned concrete containers (right) made in refreshingly crisp and modern shapes by Luna-form of Sullivan, Maine, range in height from 1 to 4 feet, and they don't blow over in the wind (the smallest weighs 50 pounds). When metal and rubber expansion plugs block the pots' drainage holes, the vessels can become miniature water gardens. The water-filled pot in the foreground holds dwarf papyrus, *Cyperus haspan*. In the background, *Canna* 'Pretoria' grows in potting mix.

garden
TOUR

The California climate encourages thoughts of the Mediterranean: the cooling pleasures of water, plants that can withstand the heat of the summer sun. So when owners Laura and David Perry asked for only two things in their Marin County garden—privacy and flower beds you could wander through as well as admire from inside the house—San Francisco–based landscape designer Scott Colombo came up with a modern American adaptation of an Italian garden.

Colombo plans his gardens around permanent structures—walls, paths, trellises—and then plants lavishly to smudge the lines. The area surrounding the house was small (40 by 130 feet) and had an awkward slope; it needed a framework of walls to keep the world at bay and terraces to create level rooms on the site. So the designer's first act was to give the property a substantial boundary. He installed a 6-foot-high front wall made of stone, *(continued on page 86)*

ROMANCING THE STONE
Stone arches lead the eye down a path that travels through three small garden rooms toward the door to the driveway. The solidity of the walls, made of Napa Valley basalt, is softened by lavish roses and luxuriant vines, while the geometry of the cobblestone paths is loosened by mown grass and sprays of lavender.

Living Rooms

Among the many roses in the garden is the sweet-scented David Austin shrub rose, *Rosa* 'Gertrude Jekyll', which dangles its blooms over chamomile and thyme (opposite top). Landscape designer Scott Colombo (opposite bottom) leans against a stone arch that opens into the view garden, with its parterre of rosemary, santolina, and white standard-trained 'Gourmet Popcorn' roses. Laura Perry joins her children in the entry garden (left).

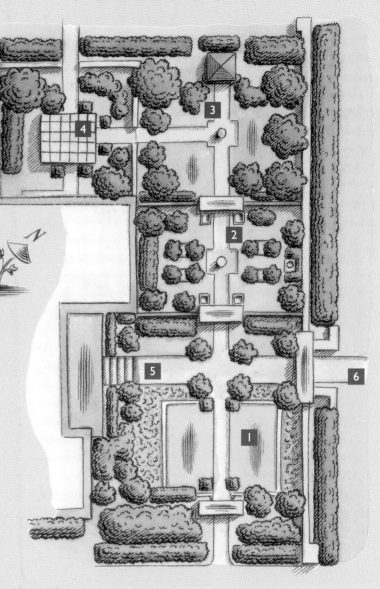

Garden Plan

Once Colombo had installed the boundaries around the property, he divided the garden into four distinct enclaves connected by a path of cobblestones and mown grass.

1. Entry garden
2. View garden
3. Meadow
4. Dining terrace
5. House entrance
6. To street

(continued from page 82) just inside a 16-foot hedge of sheared coast redwood. "A hedge alone doesn't feel as solid," he explains, "or as enclosing. And with plants creeping over it, stone instantly seems ancient."

As did the gardeners of the Mediterranean, Colombo chose to use native rock, Napa Valley basalt, which cost less than material shipped from farther afield. Next, he divided the garden into a series of four enclaves, defining them with three massive stone archways, as well as custom-made metal trellises cloaked in Boston ivy, honeysuckle, clematis, and roses, which function as screens.

A path of cobblestones and mown grass connects the four rooms, which are graded into terraces. An entry garden is draped with the heirloom roses 'Cécile Brünner' and 'Madame Ernst Calvat'. The second open-air room, which can be viewed from the dining room, holds parterres of rosemary and santolina and white standard-trained 'Gourmet Popcorn' roses. There is a third room, planted as a meadow, and, off the kitchen, a dining terrace with a pergola covered in *Polygonum aubertii* (silver lace vine) and white 'Lace Cascade' roses.

The garden also recognizes the importance of sculpture, but in its own modern way. Concrete orbs, resting on the grass or punctuating the cobblestone paths, resemble giant croquet balls and evoke a sense of play. As you wander from one room to the next, the plan of the garden unfolds. You are lured onward by the ever-present sound of water, which leads you to its source: four wall-mounted lion's-head fountains, sending their spray through the air.

The Mediterranean garden, perfectly proportioned and full of beautiful things, is always designed to please the people who own it. "We use all parts of the garden," reports Laura Perry. "It draws the family outside."

In the spring, bees are attracted to the intoxicating scent of honeysuckle and chamomile. In the autumn, the leaves of the Boston ivy and viburnum turn a bright red. And even in winter, when the roses and perennials are cut back, the stone walls and archways give the garden a feeling of age. "People enjoy gardens that look as though they've been there forever," Colombo says. "With this one, after three years, I think we're there."

ROWS OF ROSES
Boston ivy decorates the stone wall in the entry garden, while *Rosa* 'Cécile Brünner' and *R.* 'Madame Ernst Calvat' entwine over the door to the street. 'White Meidiland' standard roses and sheared boxwood punctuate the cobblestone path that runs between the garden rooms.

CHAPTER 3

BRITAIN,
ireland, and the low countries

- LISTENING TO THE LANDSCAPE

- PLANTING FOR DOMESTIC USE

- AN ECCENTRIC SENSE OF WHIMSY

- THE COLLECTING IMPULSE

- THE VIRTUE OF NATURALISM

When Henry VIII redid the gardens at Hampton Court, he decorated the rectangular enclosures with heraldic beasts—197 "dragownes, lyones, grewhoundes, harttes, Innycornes," bulls, griffins, and leopards—which held his coat of arms and that of his queen, who was, unfortunately, Anne Boleyn. Presumably, when Anne lost her head, the king changed the shields, though it's nice to think he might instead have used that old gardener's trick of training vines to cover his mistakes. Whatever the fate of the shields, the beasts of Hampton Court show the English desire to put everything into a garden as surely as Versailles illustrated the French willingness to take everything out. ■ In France, the overall effect was more important than the parts. In England, it was the delight in the individual—a newly discovered plant or an ancient gnarled tree—that dominated design, leading to landscapes where the parts shaped the whole. Though the gardens of England have had their fads and fancies, they always show the English pleasure in, and respect for, that which is individual and eccentric. ■ In the first part of the 17th century, the English did make a move toward copying French formalism. But later, while their friends across the Channel were reading Descartes and being rational, the English were executing a king, fighting a civil war, enduring the Cromwellian Protectorate, the Plague, the Great Fire of London, and the Restoration. With what breath they had left, they forced James II into exile and invited William of Orange to take the throne. ■ By the end of that exhausting century, the passion for things French had gone. Thanks to William, it was the Dutch connection that mattered, and though relations between the two nations had not always been peaceful, the Low Countries had been a crucial source of food, plants, and seeds. Exiled

Huguenots, who had lived in Holland until forced out by the war with Spain, had brought Dutch habits to England. They were leaders in the Florists' movement. (The Florists were not people who set up shop and sold bouquets, but gardeners who bred and showed certain flowers—primula, dianthus, and tulips among them.) Without them, there might have been none of the oh-so-English watercress sandwiches, since before the Huguenots gave them culinary status, both watercress and asparagus were considered medicinal herbs in England. Even the admonition to eat your spinach is due to the Dutch. John Parkinson, author of the 1629 book *Paradisi in Sole Paradisus Terrestris*, passed on the Dutch recipe for cooking spinach: "Stew the herb in a pot or pipkin without any other moisture than its own, and after the moisture is a little pressed from it. . .put butter and a little spice unto it and make therewith a dish that many delight to eat of." ■ The grand canals, the clipped hedges, and the orangeries did come to England, but under the influence of the domestic Dutch they lacked the cool majesty of Versailles. One suspects that, William of Orange or no, the English would have taken geometrical formalism and given it a shape of their own. When a young man from Basel visited England's royal palace of Nonsuch in 1599, he found it packed with topiary: "There were all manner of shapes, men and women, half men and half horse, sirens, serving-maids with baskets, French lilies and delicate crenellations all round made from dry twigs bound together and the aforesaid evergreen quick-set shrubs, or entirely of rosemary, all true to the life, and so cleverly and amusingly interwoven, mingled and grown together, trimmed and arranged picture-wise, that their equal would be difficult to find." A nation so in love with fantasy would never lose of it

elements of **british** garden style

wild garden A term popularized by William Robinson, whose 1870 book, *The Wild Garden* (illustration, opposite), quickly became a classic. "It has nothing to do with the old idea of the 'Wilderness,'" he wrote, but of learning to let hardy perennials naturalize and to benefit from "beautiful accidents": a rose scrambling up a catalpa tree, or larkspurs flourishing in a field.

ha-ha Supposedly first used in France, the ha-ha now seems totally English. A deep ditch (which is, in effect, a sunken fence) it keeps the cows from the corn without interrupting the flow of the landscape. Invisible from a distance, it presumably got its name when people caught themselves as they were about to fall in and uttered a surprised but relieved "ha-ha!"

cottage garden A style of romantic planting that combines the practical with the poetic and makes a lush garden of a small, enclosed space. Fruits and vegetables are intermingled with old-fashioned flowers; roses and honeysuckles climb the porch next to runner beans; and fruit trees are grown as espaliers against a fence or wall.

folly A whimsical structure that lightens up the garden, a folly can be anything from a red lacquer Chinese temple where the family takes tea to a garden shed shaped like a ship to a re-creation of a Gothic ruin, brooding atop a craggy hill.

border A bed, longer than it is wide, where a variety of flowers and shrubs are planted together for mass effect. The herbaceous border is usually planted with perennials, although annuals or potted plants sunk into the soil may be used to fill the gaps. Gertrude Jekyll created the style we favor today: planting in drifts using different heights and textures, and blending colors together into a harmonious whole.

landscape park In the 18th century the idea that a garden should suit its site replaced the earlier view that the site should be cleared and leveled to suit the garden. Landscape gardeners of the period banished rigidly geometric parterres and replaced them with rolling parkland, groves of trees, and a lake with a classical temple or two.

listening to the landscape

In 1731 the poet Alexander Pope gave a motto to the movement that was changing the look of the English countryside: "Consult the genius of the place in all." This dictum, still a favorite of gardeners, involved studying the lay of the land, not flattening it, and allowing trees to take their natural form instead of shearing them into assorted shapes. Topiary, in fact, was one of the prime targets of Pope and his contemporaries, who did their part to embarrass English gardeners into getting rid of the rigid geometry of the classical garden.

"Our Trees rise in Cones, Globes and Pyramids," wrote Joseph Addison in *The Spectator*. "I would rather look upon a Tree, and all its Luxuriancy and Diffusion of Boughs and Branches, than when it is thus cut and trimm'd into a mathematical Figure."

No one, not even a gardener, likes to be thought old-fashioned, and gradually the style changed as the masters of the English landscape—William Kent, Lancelot "Capability" Brown, and Humphry Repton—swept the flowers and topiary from around the house, replacing them with expansive lawns and meadows rolling down to lakes and woods.

The landscape gardeners may have pledged their troth to Mother Nature, but they were not above acting as Mother's helper—planting a forest here, digging a lake where none had been before. In their ardor, they created the countryside that inspired the romantic poets and so influenced a young American landscape gardener and writer named Andrew Jackson Downing that their ideas crossed the Atlantic, to flourish in the great urban parks of the United States.

LAY OF THE LAND
Scotney Castle (above) in Kent is an outstanding example of the picturesque garden style that was the culmination of the landscape movement. Opposite: The grounds at Stowe in Buckinghamshire were originally planned by Charles Bridgeman. "Capability" Brown became Stowe's head gardener when he was only 25.

CLASSICISM, BRITISH STYLE

The grounds of Stourhead in Wiltshire were laid out by Henry Hoare II during the height of the mid-18th-century landscape movement. After damming the River Stour to create a lake, Hoare decorated its shores with classical temples set among trees and shrubs. Winding paths ascend the hillsides, and an enormous folly on the edge of the estate offers views of the surrounding countryside.

99

planting for domestic use

By 1557, when Thomas Tusser wrote his rhymed advice to farmers, *A Hundred Good Points of Husbandry*, the contents of the cottage garden were already in place. Tusser listed everything from pumpkins to parsley to primroses as belonging in a kitchen garden: 20 plants for salads and sauces, 21 strewing herbs to rid the house of pests, roses for syrup, fruits for the still room. It's easy to visualize Tusser's garden: roses growing next to the rounceval peas, elegant artichokes, tansy looming behind rows of sweet-smelling lavender, and flowers, too—columbines, carnations, marigolds, hollyhocks.

The ingredients were there, but it took the landscape movement of the 18th century to bring the cottage garden into fashion. When the owners of large estates took down the garden walls to make their landscape parks, they discovered ramshackle cottages spoiling their views. The meaner sort of landlord knocked them down; kinder ones built new and better housing out of sight. This disruption of the poor led reformers to devise plans for ideal cottages; before long, what had been a hovel had developed social cachet.

By the early 19th century the middle class was building its own elegant cottages—and gardens to go with them. Blowsy, abundant, fragrant, they were an offshoot of the romantic era in landscaping. Styles come and go, and the Victorians disdained the cottage garden, digging up old plants to make room for exotic imports. But on rural back roads, the cottage garden remained, with its gooseberries and grapes, sorrel for soup, and the intoxicating scent of honeysuckle and rose.

FRAMING THE KITCHEN GARDEN Glass cloches (above) served as cold frames in the old-fashioned kitchen garden. Opposite: In the 19th-century walled kitchen garden of Glin Castle in County Limerick, Ireland, beds of cosmos, lupines, and nicotiana provide cutting flowers, while four 95-square-foot beds contain artichokes, sea kale, rhubarb, and other vegetables.

ACRES OF EDIBLES

Each spring a new combination of crops is planted in the boxwood-edged beds of the two-and-a-half-acre Victorian walled kitchen garden at West Dean in Sussex. Newly renovated after three decades of neglect, the garden now serves as a showcase of horticultural trends. A tunnel of arch-trained pear trees borders freshly dug soil where tepees are set out to hold runner beans. Rows of peas (under the bird netting), broad beans, lettuces, and strawberries are just beginning to grow. Terra-cotta forcing pots (at right) are set among sea kale and rhubarb.

103

ARTFUL NATURE
The kitchen garden gets a modern touch at a recent Chelsea Flower Show (this page), where British floral designer Stephen Woodhams centered the beds around a hipper version of the Victorian strawberry cage and filled galvanized-steel pots with marigolds (*Tagetes patula*) and rosemary. Herbs, edible flowers, and vegetables peacefully coexist in a space no bigger than an urban backyard. Opposite: Art is in the eye of the gardener, who can see beauty in the multicolored, veined leaves of the Brussels sprout.

the **professional** gardener

In English novels, the gardener was usually Scottish and always difficult. Did the mistress want to fill the house with roses? The gardener wanted them on the bush. Did the master want to cut a tree? The gardener glowered.

The gardener got away with it because the master knew nothing and the gardener knew all: how to save the seeds and when to sow them, how to graft the fruit and vine, what muck was best to feed the soil, when to spread lime and when to add peat. An immense amount of knowledge and an equal amount of labor went into creating a glorious garden. And both master and mistress understood that.

The head gardener of a large estate directed the under-gardeners and the gardener's boys; ran the heated glasshouses, which produced cut flowers and out-of-season fruit; oversaw the kitchen garden, the rose garden, the perennial garden, the orchard, and the park; and supervised the bedding out and the tossing out, the pleaching of the hedges and the pruning of the trees.

Since 1977 there has been a Professional Gardeners' Guild in England, an official version of an unofficial union that has been handing down plant lore and knowledge for more than a thousand years. Even the tools sketched by John Evelyn in the mid-1600s are the ones we use today: three-pronged hoes, grafting knives, spades, rakes, mattocks, forks, and bird scarers. What container gardener wouldn't be happy to have the stretcherlike apparatus used to carry potted plants from place to place?

Few people can employ one gardener, much less the hundred or so who once tended Warley Place in Essex. But the lore of the professional gardener lives on, though there are few suburbanites who would adopt the ancient way of gauging when it was warm enough to plant: The gardener pulled down his pants and sat on the ground.

TOOLS OF THE GARDEN TRADE
Tom Wall (this page) stands with his sidekicks in the 2-acre walled kitchen garden at Glin Castle near Limerick, where he has been head gardener for more than 20 years. Opposite: Three centuries of gardening paraphernalia are displayed at the Museum of Garden History in London. The only museum of its kind, it also houses a treasury of rare plants.

an eccentric sense of whimsy

While the French garden is shaped with a stylish restraint, the charm of the English garden lies in the quirkiness of its creators. The shapers of the romantic rural landscape had no sooner perfected their craft than another generation came along to give nature a wilder look. Their style came to be called picturesque, and their landscapes gave precedence to dead trees and raging streams.

"It is almost comic to set aside a quarter of one's garden to be melancholy in," remarked Horace Walpole as the vogue for the picturesque gained hold, culminating in the construction of stone grottoes and hermitages hidden in the woods. One visitor described a hermit's cell made of the roots of trees: "[T]he floor is paved with pebbles, there is a couch made of matting, and little wooden stools, a table with a manuscript on it, a pair of spectacles, a leathern bottle. . .everything that you might imagine necessary for a recluse." Everything you might imagine if you were a wealthy, slightly eccentric Englishman.

Estate owners built houses in trees, houses lined with seashells, Greek temples, and Chinese bridges. In the mid-19th century a gentleman named Sir Charles Isham peopled his rock garden with gnomes, starting a fad that persists today. All of these whimsical additions were in the grand tradition of British gardening; as far back as the 17th century shank bones of sheep were used to edge garden beds.

In most countries a folly is something to regret. In England it is to be indulged in and enjoyed, for what is a garden without a bit of fantasy: a Gothic ruin, an Indian tepee, a four-poster bed shaped from boxwood?

FANCIFUL FORMS
At Larchill (above) in County Kildare, Ireland, a crumbling folly was built to provide a hideout for the owner, a hunter who feared reincarnation as a fox. Opposite: In Scotland a delightfully unexpected collection of topiary grows alongside a stream at the Tormore Distillery, south of Grantown on Spey. The fantastical shapes are the work of a distillery employee.

ORNAMENTAL ODDITIES

Pomona, the goddess of fruits, is not an ancient statue carved from marble but a modern mascot made of concrete (this page). She guards the orchard at Charleston in East Sussex, home of Vanessa Bell, who along with her sister, Virginia Woolf, was a member of the Bloomsbury Group. Opposite: The thatched *cottage orné* ("ornamental cottage") on the grounds of Kilfane Glen in County Kilkenny, Ireland, was part of a wild garden constructed around 1800.

the collecting impulse

Most people have never heard of David Douglas, even those who use his name every Christmas when they buy a Douglas fir. One of the earliest of the 19th-century plant collectors, Douglas roamed the American West on foot, canoe, and horseback and sent back to England not only the famous fir but more than 200 other species.

The Victorians were not the first plant explorers to harvest foreign fields. "I have already an orange tree, and if the price be not much I pray you procure for me a lemon, a pomegranate, and a myrt [myrtle] tree," wrote one Englishman to a friend in Paris in 1562. What set the Victorians apart was the volume of what they found.

Robert Fortune sailed to the Orient for the first time in 1843, and by the end of his career he had not only smuggled tea plants out of China, making possible tea plantations in India, but had introduced into England *Jasminum nudiflorum, Weigela florida, Viburnum macrocephalum, Rhododendron obtusum, Dicentra spectabilis,* and many others. Even Victorian women entered the lists. Marianne North traveled all over the world—America, Japan, Java, Australia, South Africa, India—to do botanical illustrations of nearly 1,000 species.

Orchids, chrysanthemums, camellias, dahlias, petunias: hundreds of plants flooded English gardens. The new discoveries were grown in greenhouses, placed in beds en masse to bloom, and then moved out— a practice known as "bedding out." Gardens conform not only to their site but to the culture that creates them. In the 19th century, England conquered the world and brought it home to the garden.

WORLD TRAVELERS
Among the horticultural treasures brought back to England by 19th-century explorers were dahlias (above), which had earlier migrated from Mexico to Spain. Opposite: In a photo-graph, circa 1880, the head gardener at Heligan House in Cornwall stands with gunnera. Known for the plant-collecting habits of its 19th-century owners, Heligan recently under-went a major restoration.

SEARCHING FOR THE EXOTIC
Artist Marianne North (this page), shown at her easel, began her epic journeys around the world in 1871. The botanical illustrations she painted during 16 years of travel are now housed in the Royal Botanic Gardens at Kew. Opposite: The visually impressive Turk's cap lily, *Lilium martagon*, was brought to England from Asia Minor, one of many popular destinations for Victorian plant collectors. One explorer, Ernest Henry Wilson, brought back so many plants from China—some 3,000—that he has gone down in history as "Chinese" Wilson.

the virtue of naturalism

In the late 19th century William Robinson, editor of 3 gardening magazines and 18 books on gardening, issued a call to respect the integrity of the plant. "The best way in gardening is always to grow the flowers that thrive without great labour in the soil we have," he wrote in 1883 in *The English Flower Garden*—advice that, in the Victorian era, amounted to heresy.

During the preceding century England had been entranced with the exotic plants being discovered around the globe. Their novelty and brilliant colors led gardeners to raise them in greenhouses and move them into the garden, a process that Robinson derided.

An Irishman, Robinson had begun his professional life as a gardener's boy, and he preached the virtues of the wildflower, taught readers to let spring bulbs naturalize in lawn or meadow, and advocated woodland gardens.

He was helped in his crusade by Gertrude Jekyll, who championed naturalistic planting in rural cottage gardens. An artist whose failing eyesight had made her abandon the paintbrush for the spade, Jekyll carried on Robinson's ideas in the books she wrote, in the almost 350 gardens she helped design, and in her own renowned garden at Munstead Wood in Surrey, where the perennial border was 200 feet long and 14 feet wide.

"Show me your spaces and I will tell you what plants to get for them," she told people who asked for advice. And she also wrote, "As in much else, one must watch what happens in one's own garden."

PERENNIAL INSPIRATION
Gertrude Jekyll in 1920 (above), when she was 77 years old. With William Robinson, she rejected the system of bedding out and taught gardeners how to use plants of varying heights and colors to create long perennial borders. Opposite: Jekyll's garden at Munstead Wood has recently been restored.

TAMING THE WILD
In the gardens designed
by Gertrude Jekyll at Vann
in Surrey, the pond at
the bottom of the stream
(this page) is formed by a
dam planted with ferns,
wild irises, dogwoods, and
gunnera. Opposite: In the
stream border, Jekyll subtly
wove together plants,
water, and paths to effect
a gradual transition from
the manicured formality
at one end to the shaggy
wildness at the other. The
stream runs between a
formal, yew-lined corridor
and is bordered with spiky
Sisyrinchium striatum, white
foxgloves, and *Santolina
chamaecyparissus*. "Wild
gardening is . . . delightful,"
Jekyll wrote, but "so difficult to do well."

PAINTER'S PALETTE
Nori and Sandra Pope
(opposite) have created a
colorist's delight in the
300-year-old garden at
Hadspen House in Somer-
set. Like Gertrude Jekyll,
they take a painter's view
of the border. "When
confronted by a continu-
ous color, you stop seeing
it so intensely," says Nori,
explaining the importance
of patches of blue in the
yellow border. Flowers
and foliage in rich shades
of maroon, plum, and red-
violet (this page) are set
against a lichen-cloaked
terra-cotta wall.

121

GARDEN PLAN

The Popes' garden is entered through a semicircular wall, with color flowing along the curve in both directions. Dark red-violets change to magenta, then into crimsons, scarlets, oranges, and yellows.

1. Entering the secluded garden, visitors are surrounded by a wall of brick capped with limestone.

2. In the curve of the wall lie the vegetable beds. Their distinct order, form, and texture are juxtaposed with the riot of color climbing the walls and spilling onto the paths from the shallow borders.

3. On either side of the central walks are shrubs with plum and gray foliage. Against the one straight wall are borders of hydrangeas and rodgersias.

4. From the garden bench, the visitor looks down the double hosta walk, a tapestry of greens, blues, and golds. Further down the path, yellow borders frame the third opening in the wall.

BOTH COLORFUL AND BOUNTIFUL
In the Popes' kitchen garden each bed can be planted, weeded, and harvested from all sides. Paths frame rectangular beds and create a dense patchwork of color and texture against the curved wall. Culinary herbs are grown in the bed that follows the line of path and wall; vegetables like 'Bull's Blood' beets and ruby chard provide bursts of bright color.

LAVISH BORDERS
On either side of a brick path, Dutch garden designer Piet Oudolf created borders that feature plants in an extravagant mix of sizes, shapes, and textures. Low-growing *Sedum telephium* 'Matrona', *Origanum* 'Rosenkuppel', and *Molinia caerulea* form an understory to the medium-height *Echinacea purpurea* 'Alba', *Verbascum chaixii* 'Album', and *Phlox paniculata* 'Rosa Pastell'. Vertical structure is provided by *Veratrum californicum*, *Angelica gigas*, *Veronicastrum virginicum* 'Fascination', *Echinops sphaerocephalus*, and drooping tufts of *Miscanthus sinensis* 'Flamingo'.

125

bringing it
HOME

Though we may love Great Britain's perennial borders and yearn to plant on a chalky down, the reality is that in much of the United States the climate and soil make it impossible to produce a faithful copy of the English garden. Delphiniums in the Delta? Old climbing roses in Burlington, Vermont? Possible, perhaps, but only with herculean effort—so, being American we have learned to improvise.

Thomas Jefferson's Monticello sits on a mountainside gazing down on an American version of a landscape park. A folly in the form of a temple would look out of place on a suburban lot, but what about a garden shed turned upside down? The profusion of blooms that marks the cottage garden can be seen from Los Angeles to Miami, and daffodils naturalized on sloping banks edge highways across the United States. By adjusting to our surroundings, we have Americanized the English garden.

Azalea Woods

Henry Francis du Pont created the spectacular gardens at Winterthur in Delaware with the aid of landscape architect Marian Cruger Coffin. A fan of both William Robinson and Gertrude Jekyll, du Pont preferred a fluid style attuned to the local terrain and the native flora. Jekyll's books made du Pont appreciate the importance of color as an organizing force, and the rosy lavender of a *Rhododendron mucronulatum* is a hue he wove through many areas of the garden. The Azalea Woods (left) display the artful structure that du Pont based on layering of the native forest: high canopy, understory, and low-growing ground cover. He originally started planting rare Kurume azaleas to fill in gaps left by blighted chestnut trees.

127

Natural Majesty

While England had to create a picturesque landscape, Alaska has one ready-made. The Eagle River and Chugach Mountains form a dramatic backdrop to the gardens of Donald and Susan Brusehaber. "After 25 years," they say, "we maintain a balance that's not too carefully weeded or trimmed—and looks as though it was always there." Native cow parsnip, wild geraniums, and daisies thrive among the grasses of the "beach" garden. The Brusehabers have sowed many other native plants, including milk vetch, avens, saxifrage, and Eskimo potato (*Hedysarum alpinum*). In another part of the garden, there is even a folly: a gazebo made from a turn-of-the-century fishing boat turned upside down and set on posts.

The Groves of Monticello

Monticello, the 5,000-acre mountaintop estate built by Thomas Jefferson near Charlottesville, Virginia, was a working farm where he cultivated a staggering number of plants for home use and experimentation: more than 250 vegetable varieties at any one time in a 1,000-by-80-foot terraced plot, and 150 fruit trees in an 8-acre orchard. But it was also a place where Jefferson, who had toured England at the height of the romantic landscape movement, was able to create his own naturalistic landscape. At Monticello he chose to use groves of trees, curving walks, and oval flower beds instead of the formal parterres and avenues of Tuckahoe, his childhood home. An aerial view shows the vegetable garden on the right and the landscaped park surrounding the house.

DOMESTIC: COTTAGE GARDEN

Old-Fashioned Aesthetic

"I have a cottage, so I planted a traditional cottage garden," says Karen Skelton, who, with her husband, Richard Siegel, runs a pottery studio and shop in upstate New York. But it's the unexpected twists on tradition that define their aesthetic. Their border garden (left) may be filled with "old-fashioned, pretty, flowery stuff" like balloon flowers, cosmos, petunias, and buddleia, but it also includes yuccas, ornamental grasses, sedums—and a pair of spiky potted pineapples at the entrance.

Domestic Order

In the Bucks County, Pennsylvania, cottage garden of Hunter Runnette and Mark Vandenbosch (right), raised beds edged with roof slates hold poles for peas and beans, as well as rows of lettuce, kohlrabi, cabbage, beets, squash, 12 varieties of peppers, and 6 of eggplant. Flowers grow in a garden beyond the gate. The 10-acre property also holds a grape arbor and areas for an animal population ranging from emus, peacocks, and pheasants to goats, pigs, and sheep.

New Twist on a Traditional Art

Pearl Fryar of Bishopville, South Carolina, never studied topiary. He re-invented it. His house hovers behind a landscape of trees and shrubs trained into whimsical shapes—hearts, mushrooms, letters of the alphabet, and even a 20-foot-tall fishbone of Leyland cypress. When someone gave him a book on traditional topiary, Fryar tried the conventional geometric shapes but eventually rejected them. "No, this ain't gonna work for me," he said. "I like to make a statement with lines and curves." And a statement is what he has made, with his "love" hedge (left) to welcome visitors, spirals (right), and myriad other forms. "I must have a thousand shapes here," says Fryar. "I can't start working on one plant without thinking about how it relates to the next."

Topsy-Turvy Shed

In Sonoma County, California, a pair of inventive gardeners have used salvaged treasures to create their own thoroughly modern follies. In the garden of Kathleen and John Holmes, plastic milk-carton crates wired together form the base for a cross-shaped topiary covered with *Gelsemium sempervirens*. Vines climb galvanized-steel culvert pipes (left) and stretch out on a "trellis" made from commercial radio antennae. But what really stops visitors to the garden is the upside-down potting shed, which John assembled from cast-off windows. The shed's door is concealed in the roof. Once opened (right), it reveals a functional space for storage, starting seedlings, and other projects.

Babes in the Woods

It would be hard to find anyone who more closely embraced William Robinson's notion of naturalizing bulbs than did Carl Krippendorf. The son of a shoe manufacturer from Cincinnati, Krippendorf rescued 175 acres of woodland from the ax and began to plant Lob's Wood (left). He was proud to have a bulb in bloom every month of the year. Over 50 years, he planted tens of thousands of them, spreading them in vast drifts along shady trails or tucking small colonies under his beloved beech trees. Many of the little bulbs (right) still bloom in the woodland, now the Cincinnati Nature Center. Clockwise from top left: spring snowflakes (*Leucojum vernum*); *Tulipa tarda*; glory-of-the-snow (*Chionodoxa luciliae*); *Hyacinthus orientalis* var. *albulus*; Siberian squill (*Scilla siberica*); and Grecian windflower (*Anemone blanda*).

Seasonal Spectrum

On a bluff overlooking Washington's Puget Sound, Judith Prindle has followed the advice of Gertrude Jekyll to create a border featuring "the juxtaposition of rightly placed complementary colour." In the border's northwestern curve (left), Prindle uses subordinate yet complementary tones of yellow-green, such as the chartreuse of *Alchemilla mollis*, to set off the diverse pinks of the roses 'Blush Noisette', 'Slater's Crimson China', and Mary Rose. *Geranium sanguineum* and *Heuchera* 'Palace Purple' fly the team colors from May to November. Weaving a tapestry of color (right), Prindle partners the silver lace of *Helichrysum italicum* (*H. angustifolium*) with gray-green and white *Iris pallida* to reflect the hue of coastal waters and sky. Golden leaves of *Salvia officinalis* 'Icterina' and the ornamental grass *Hakonechloa macra* 'Aureola' perform a duet in another key.

The Bellevue Bays

The Bellevue Botanical Garden near Seattle, Washington, with a climate similar to England's, has a 17,000-square-foot border planted on a slope and filled with 1,000 different perennials—10,000 plants in all. Because the steep pitch of the site and a central bog made the traditional English border—laid out on both sides of a path—impossible, the Bellevue border is organized in "bays" of plants grouped by color. At the back of the pink-and-white bay (left), Joe-pye weed, *Buddleia davidii* 'Pink Delight', and *Galega officinalis* 'Lady Wilson' rise above *Agapanthus* Headbourne Hybrids, *Molinia caerulea* 'Variegata', and striped *Alstroemeria* 'Storytella'. Right: Tufts of *Stipa tenacissima* wave over a winding path, along with pink evening primrose (*Oenothera* 'Siskiyou') and lavender-blue Russian sage (*Perovskia*).

garden
TOUR

The New England gardens of Judy and Pat Murphy embrace several centuries of British landscape design and yet are as American as the sugar maple. The Murphys' home garden shares 25 acres in Lakeville, Connecticut, with Judy's business, Old Farm Nursery. There is a sunny flower border, a shade garden, a formal kitchen garden, and, farther out, a naturalistic pond.

The view from the vegetable garden over the New England countryside, with its endless blue sky and rolling hills flecked with red barns, rivals any created by the 18th-century devotees of the landscape movement. "To be so intimate with nature, with soil and frost and sun and rain, is amazing. It connects you to something larger, gives you a way of seeing something much bigger than yourself," says Murphy of a landscape she describes as "all knotty and bumpy, with fantastic views."

Murphy's garden begins with a profusion of roses climbing a picket fence. Inside, the perennial border—which undulates around *(continued on page 148)*

Close-Up and Long View

Judy and Pat Murphy (opposite top) stand at the entrance to their kitchen garden, flanked by two antique chimney pots. Honeysuckle *Lonicera* x *Brownii* 'Dropmore Scarlet' climbs steel topiary towers (opposite bottom). Along the picket fence (left) are low-growing Rugosa roses, *Crambe cordifolia*, 'Claridge Druce' geraniums, and 'Mona Lisa' and 'Stargazer' lilies. An iron tuteur adds height and humor. Beyond the fence, low-maintenance islands of daylilies, miscanthus, and dwarf conifers such as white pine, scotch pine, and blue spruce lead the eye out onto a landscape as romantic as an English park.

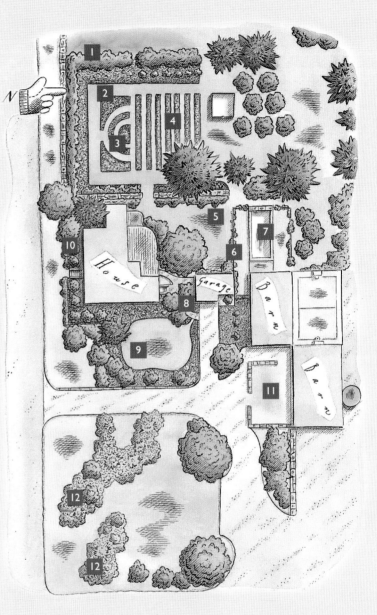

Garden Plan

1. Arborvitae hedge
2. Annuals
3. Roses
4. Vegetables
5. Backyard
6. Grape arbor
7. Swimming pool
8. Shade garden
9. Fenced garden
10. Foundation plantings
11. Garden ornaments
12. Grasses and evergreens

(continued from page 144) the lawn—looks like an old-fashioned cottage garden. Only later do you notice another English touch: a sense of whimsy, seen, for instance, in the huge, outrageous leaves of a cardoon that lurk among the peonies and roses.

"Our garden happened bit by bit," says Murphy, who was trained as a landscape architect. If a nursery shrub came off the truck with a broken limb, she would stick it in her yard. Distinct garden areas evolved as she searched for solutions to everyday problems. "The kids were small, so I needed a fenced yard for them to play in," she explains. "I wound up experimenting with a perennial border in there. I wanted privacy from the road, so I planted a row of fast-growing arborvitae. It's the usual stuff people deal with: I wanted fresh produce, so I set aside an area for edibles; I needed a way to get from the garage to the back of the house, so I laid a brick path and began planting around it."

This Everyman approach has produced spectacular results. But then, the gardener is guided by Murphy's Laws:

Choose a theme. "Don't put an Italian grotto on the side, an English border out back, and a replica of Versailles in your front yard." You can meld motifs, says Murphy, if they're filtered through a single, strong vision.

Repeat plants and colors. "If you buy one of everything, you'll wind up with nothing, no impact. But choose three of one thing, five of another, and you can really see the plants."

Think in terms of architecture. "Whether it's one room, half a room, or just a narrow hallway, a space needs walls. It should be anchored, with entrances and exits."

Don't overlook annuals. "Plant only perennials, and you're going to have bald spots at different times. Annuals flower all season long, and some will self-seed. Mix a few in, and you'll always have something in bloom."

BORDER LINES
One side of the kitchen garden is bordered by a stone wall, while another is open to the rolling hills of the surrounding Connecticut countryside. Terra-cotta chimney pots create an unconventional entrance to the garden.

FRANCE

It took Nicolas Fouquet, minister of finance under King Louis XIV, 20 years, 16 million pounds, and the services of 18,000 workers to bring his estate, Vaux-le-Vicomte, to a point of perfection. Naturally, he wanted to show it off. On August 17, 1661, he assembled 6,000 guests for an extravagant fete in honor of Louis XIV. Two weeks later Fouquet was in jail, imprisoned by the king, who suspected it was his own coffers that had provided the money for this "luxe insolent et audacieux." ■ Fouquet remained in prison for 19 years before death released him, but his celebration had changed the landscape of France. Not only did Louis XIV help himself to Fouquet's garden statuary and a thousand orange trees, which he shipped off to Versailles; but he also made off with the gardener, André Le Nôtre. ■ More than any other person, Le Nôtre is responsible for the serene, formal gardens we associate with France. With Vaux-le-Vicomte, Versailles, Chantilly, Saint-Cloud, and the many other estates designed by the master gardener and his pupils, the French garden, once based on the medieval model of small, enclosed plots planted close to the house, spread out into the countryside and became the landscape that visitors to France admire today. ■ Trees and shrubs were clipped into balls, rectangles, or triangles; low hedges outlined beds laid out in geometric shapes or fancy scrolls, which were then filled with colored earth. (One of Le Nôtre's peculiarities was that he did not like flowers.) These grand 17th-century gardens were to be admired from on high, seen from windows or from terraces surrounding the châteaux, as overlords and their ladies surveyed the patterns they had made on the land. ■ The gardens were laid out around a central axis, shaded and defined by trees planted in perfect pairs on either side, disappearing two by two into the distance. While other countries clamored for the new plants that explorers were shipping

back to Europe, France had the soothing repetition of yew, linden, hornbeam, and box-wood, plants able to survive the pruning necessary to keep a triangle from burgeoning into a square. Instead of bright colors, there was the subtle play of light and shadow. Instead of tumbling streams, there were still waters, *miroirs d'eau*, contained in pools or canals, reflecting clouds and sky. ■ These were gardens based on the rational notion that man could control nature, a landscape bred by the age of Descartes and Pascal; it would be almost a hundred years before Rousseau would preach the dangerous doctrine that man was a wild child. Gardens for the rational, but also for the rich: It took money to hire the labor to move the trees, build the terraces, and do the constant planting and pruning that linear gardens require. At Versailles, a river was diverted, a lake emptied, and 37,000 acres of marshland drained to provide water for the garden's 1,400 foun-tains. Even that was not enough, and only the fountains near the château flowed all the time. Others were turned on by runners who darted ahead to make still waters dance as the Sun King came into view. ■ As a revolution was to show, not all of France was given to rationality and few had access to riches. Beyond the magnificent formal gar-dens, there remained an older style of gardening: the *jardin de curé*, or "priest's garden," where a nation that made an art of food grew the ingredients that brought magic to the mundane. In the jardin de curé, shaped by a desire for abundance rather than design, a cabbage was not a circle to anchor a square but food to put in the pot. ■ Le Nôtre, despite his association with the king, came from just such a background. Both his father and his grandfather were gardeners, and when the king decorated him at the end of his long career, Le Nôtre, with humor and humility, chose as a coat of arms what would be found in any jardin de curé: a spade surrounded by slugs and topped with cabbage leaves.

elements of **french** garden style

allée An avenue symmetrically bordered on either side by trees or hedges. One allée may form the primary axis in a garden, or several allées may be arranged in lines radiating out from the château or crossing at right angles. The allée is sometimes replaced by a *miroir d'eau*, a pool or long canal whose still water offers a reflection of both château and sky.

parterre Literally, "on the ground." A level space in the garden laid out with beds contained within a hedge, commonly of boxwood, but occasionally of shrubby herbs like lavender, rosemary, or rue. The beds, which can be as simple as a rectangle or as elaborate as a fleur-de-lis, are now usually filled with flowers, but in the 17th century the pattern was more often created by filling the spaces with gravel or colored sand.

potager From the French *potage*, or "soup." The potager is a kitchen garden where herbs, vegetables, and flowers are all grown together. The fashion dates back to medieval monasteries, where the need to be self-sufficient demanded a steady supply of soup vegetables (usually alliums and beans) as well as herbs and flowers for flavoring, medicinal purposes, and dyes.

espalier A labor-intensive technique by which a fruit tree or vine is trained on a lattice, on wires, or against a wall or fence to create geometric shapes. The most common shapes for the espalier are the palmette (which includes the fan and the candelabra) and the cordon (which can be vertical, horizontal, or angled to form a lattice). The pear tree shown opposite, from Saint-Jean-de-Beauregard, is an example of a horizontal cordon.

jardin de curé Literally, the "priest's garden." The *jardin de curé* is the antithesis of the formal, geometric French garden. Its form—as overflowing as the cottage garden—has been shaped by its function: providing flowers for the altar, vegetables for the kitchen, and herbs for flavoring and medicinal use.

bosquet Defined in an early 18th-century gardening book as "small Compartments...form'd of Trees, Shrubs, or tall large growing plants," bosquets at Versailles were the sheltered outdoor rooms opening off the garden's central axis where Louis XIV held elaborate alfresco parties.

the power of geometry

A nation that has devised 50 ways to make a soufflé and as many methods of shaping a dress is not going to be daunted by the difficulty of creating gardens based on the straight line, the circle, the triangle, and the square. Just as the rise of the soufflé or the drape of the dress depends on its proportions, so does the order of the formal garden.

Dézallier d'Argenville, a contemporary of Louis XIV, set out the principles of formal gardens with the certainty of a schoolboy reciting that an isosceles triangle has two equal sides. His 1709 treatise, which passed on the precepts learned from one of Le Nôtre's pupils, stated that the length of the garden should be one and a half times its breadth and that there should be two principal walks at right angles. The area directly in front of the house should be kept open, the width of this space equaling the height of the house from ground level to cornice. But the main gardens "should not lay too open," d'Argenville wrote. "The pleasure of a Garden is to have the View stopt in certain places, that you may be led on with Delight to see the more agreeable Parts of it." And his last rule, one that gardeners through all ages and in all places agree on: "A Garden should always look bigger than it really is."

The French are experts at optical illusion. A trick of perspective like shortening the height of trees and hedges as they move away from the house can make the central axis look longer than it actually is. And plane thinking—having the garden exist at several different levels through the use of steps, terraces, arbors, and container-grown plants—increases the feeling of space by elevating the gaze.

OPTICAL ILLUSION
A *tonnelle*, or bower, of hornbeam (above) leads the eye on and raises the height of the formal garden at the 16th-century Château de Chamerolles. Opposite: It may look like simple geometry, but in Paris's Parc de Bercy, the square island in a circular pool is also practical, allowing for the preservation of 19th-century buildings that once housed the city's wine market.

ORNAMENTAL PATTERNS

In the gardens of Villandry in the Loire Valley, the artichoke is art. The boxwood-edged gardens are arranged on three levels. Of the two ornamental gardens, one is planted in bright colors in parterres shaped like swords, daggers, masks, and crosses; the other is planted in subtler shades in parterres shaped like stylized musical instruments. But the most famous feature at Villandry is the intricate potager, laid out in geometric patterns that acknowledge the beauty of the things we eat.

FRAMING THE VIEW
Perspective plays an important part in drawing the eye down a long allée of perfectly aligned and clipped linden trees adjacent to the Grand Canal at Versailles (this page). Opposite: At the 12th-century Prieuré Notre-Dame-d'Orsan, in the Berry region of central France, an oval *oeil-de-boeuf* ("bull's-eye window") clipped from a tunnel of cherry trees frames a herd of grazing cattle.

163

AXIAL SYMMETRY

In redesigning the Palais-Royal courtyard garden in Paris in 1992, American garden designer Mark Rudkin revived the basic plan of 1730, with its symmetrical rows of clipped, arching linden trees and a central round fountain. He added four small "scented garden sitting rooms," with simple, powerful plantings of heliotrope and nicotiana, surrounded by multi-colored raised beds of such annuals as blue petunias, white cosmos, lemon yellow marigolds, and New Guinea impatiens with white and pinkish flowers.

structured abundance

Early in the season, the vegetable garden is as contained as a game of ticktacktoe. A thin line of leeks, a square of ruby red chard, a circle of young squash—independent kingdoms connected only by the gardener, who passes from one to another, sprinkling water and wielding the hoe. The cool days of spring give way to the long days of summer. The earth heats up and the boundaries blur. Now squash vines are twining their tendrils around the stalks of chard, marching through the carrots, and sending runners down the mounds of earth that blanch the leeks.

In an ordinary vegetable garden, it is time to call in the peacemaker—the tiller, the shears, or the hoe—to head off the invading forces before the kingdom of carrots succumb. But the French, whose combination of precision and style has made an art of the ordinary, find such solutions too dull. The red lettuce 'Rouge d'Hiver' will be laid out in checkerboard squares next to the pale green butterhead, and the whole will be bound in place by a low border of bronze calendulas, whose petals will add color to a salad. The tomato vines will have no chance to creep or mat. They will rise vertically, trained to a bamboo tepee, where their red fruit will catch the sun for earlier ripening. There will be marigolds between the rows of potatoes, an allée of dark red dahlias, fruit trees trained on wires (a graceful shape but also a way of keeping their branches from shading out the sun). The French are doing what they always do: practical magic, as old as the mystical chants of the priests and monks whose gardens also yielded the herbs to heal, the food to nourish, and the flowers to place on the altars of their churches.

TRAINING NATURE
In the *potager aromatique* at the Prieuré Notre-Dame-d'Orsan (above), herb-filled borders and a colorful array of squash and pumpkins are contained in 24-inch-deep raised beds. Opposite: Many of the gardens at Orsan are enclosed by the same easy-to-train hornbeam used for more formal parterres. Gardener Gilles Guillot ties a young branch to a trellis.

GOOD LOOKS AND GOOD PRODUCE
The potager at Orsan (this page) would make any medieval monk proud, with its maze of plots bearing vegetables, herbs, fruits, and flowers. Height in the garden is provided by espaliered plum trees, quince trees trained over lattice niches, and grapevines that fill the quadrants opening off the central path. Opposite: Tomatoes are tied on rustic trellises, where they not only thrive from the added exposure to sun but are easier to pick and grow out of range of creatures that crawl on the ground.

the sensuality of fragrance

A visitor returning from France carries not only the visual image of the landscape but also its fleeting smells: resinous rosemary clinging to the clothes after a walk up a dry, rocky hill; lavender, as sharp and light as a hug from an elderly aunt; the heavy sweetness of orange blossoms, a scent that so enraptured Louis XIV that at Versailles he had orange trees in silver tubs in all his rooms; the tantalizingly evasive violet, wrapped in a tight bunch and sold by a street vendor. The violet was the flower favored by Napoléon and Josephine—though anyone who has visited Malmaison knows how much of her heart she gave to the rose.

Fragrance tips us back in time, whether in a bouquet of blooms, in a border we brush past, or on the stopper of a cut-glass bottle—the concentrated oil stolen from the petals of a thousand flowers. When the 16th-century peasants cut the flowers in the field, they had to gather a quarter of a ton of *Lavandula stoechas* to make 2¼ pounds of the scented oil. Homemade vessels were filled with the flowers, and steam was pumped in until the vapor rose, carrying the lavender oil up and out, into a condenser, where it was skimmed from the top. Some flowers, like jasmine and tuberose, which relinquished their scent only under pressure, were spread over thin layers of grease and fat and pressed into pomades used to perfume hands and hair.

From these simple floral fragrances came the complex perfumes that are as synonymous with Paris as the deadpan models gliding down the runway in this year's version of haute couture. It is not perfume, but French perfume, a sensual, luxurious world bred from fields of flowers.

AROMATIC AIRS
For more than 400 years, the town of Grasse was the center of the French perfume industry, with acres of land turned over to cultivating lavender, roses, jonquils, and jasmine. Whether it's the irresistible perfume of *Rosa* x *centifolia* (opposite), jasmine (above), or a field of mimosa, a drive in the countryside around Grasse offers a heaven of scent.

LAVENDER FIELDS
Although lavender flowers vary in color from pale to dark purple and from white to pink, with leaves ranging from light gray to green, the cultivars of *Lavandula angustifolia,* "true lavender," produce the sweetest oil. The aromatic, woody evergreen plants are transformed for up to two months each summer into a haze of tiny blossoms, as seen in this field near Riez, Provence.

creating style with ornament

It's one thing to know that gargoyles are peering down from the upper reaches of a French cathedral. It would be quite another to discover a plaster gnome making its home in a hornbeam hedge. Silliness has no place in the classical garden, where ornaments are used to enhance, not to divert or distract. Classical statuary or fountains of marble or stone, formal benches, urns sitting gracefully atop their pedestals: These are the things that punctuate the allée or parterre, solid notes in a sylvan world that shifts with the play of sun and shade. Architects preach that ornamental motifs should never dominate a house; in the same way, the elements that furnish a garden should be in keeping with its style.

In a bosquet, the marble gods may romp, but for mortals, playfulness belongs in the potager. Who could be serious amid the rotundities of eggplants and the fecundities of squash? Certainly not the French, who may top a garden wall with a collection of ancient watering cans, old cast-iron sprinklers, or the graceful glass cloches that protect plants from frost. There are rustic benches, herbs in clay pots, low wooden barrels to center a square of lettuce and keep the roaming mint at bay, a sundial set in a patch of thyme.

Style in the potager can be an arbor of twigs or a Gothic gate, a scarecrow dressed in haute couture, a copy of the main house in miniature to provide a home for birds, a garden shed painted in trompe l'oeil—when you're not thinking classically, think like Cocteau.

FANCY FLOURISHES
When the French recently put together a project that teamed modern designers with traditional crafts-people, one result was an imaginative garden chair with bentwood ovals made of chestnut (above). Opposite: A hat trimmed on the spot with roses combines fantasy and style at the opening of L'Art du Jardin, a spring garden festival in Paris.

UPDATED CLASSICS
What could be more sensual than a bunch of peonies packed tight in a pot (this page)? Arranged by the fashionable Paris *fleuriste* Christian Tortu, the arrangement's blowsy abundance is balanced by the classical shape of an antique urn. Opposite: Working in a currently collectible style known as *faux bois* ("imitation wood"), designer Fabien Rouchoux casts concrete garden furniture, a modern take on rustic twig pieces of the past.

bringing it
HOME

Garden designer Russell Page pointed out that Le Nôtre "designed and planted his many gardens in the framework of Louis XIV's France, her architecture and decoration, her repertory of plant material, her attitude towards religion, philosophy, and social problems. . . . his gardens have style because he designed his creations inside the terms and formulas of his day."

The gardens that successfully translate French style into an American vernacular take formal geometric structure and adapt it to the terms and formulas of our modern world. Instead of stopping at a marble statue of Pan, an allée may lead to a simple garden shed. A *miroir d'eau* may be a swimming pool. Hardy native plants may bloom in the center of a boxwood-edged parterre. The formal garden demands neatness, but in return it provides structure in our busy and chaotic times. In an era when the options seem dauntingly limitless, it's a relief to have a garden where squares, circles, and lines keep it organized.

Modern Landscape

What could be more minimalist than a garden containing simple rows of peonies? It is an appropriately linear landscape for two collectors of minimalist art—Alvin and Barbara Krakow. The bushes will toe the line through the growing season, but, being peonies, the blooms will flop after a heavy rain. This decision to blur the geometric neatness of the garden by letting plants follow their natural form is typical of Michael Van Valkenburgh, the Cambridge-based landscape architect who designed the Krakows' Boston garden. The peony rows play on the classical style of the allée to impart a modern message. "Nature etches its mark on the landscape," says Van Valkenburgh, "but the designer cannot foresee all the dimensions nature will add to his design."

At Allée's End

In Robert Meltzer's eastern Long Island garden (left), ribbons of nepeta line a grass path bordered by old-fashioned pink and white shrub roses, which are underplanted with bearded iris. The small wooden building carries the silver tones of the nepeta to a higher plane and provides a focal point at the end of the allée. Meltzer has collaborated with several landscape designers on his complex of gardens, including Edwina vonGal, who designed the rose garden, and A. E. Bye, who helped draw up a master plan.

From a Distance

As manager of the garden division of New York City's Rockefeller Center, David Murbach restored the complex's roof gardens (right) to their original 1930s design. Like the 17th-century courtesans looking out on the gardens of the grand châteaux, occupants of the surrounding high-rises have a bird's-eye view of these classical parterres. "Every day, from windows on every side," says Murbach, "thousands of people stroll the gardens with their eyes."

GEOMETRY: PARTERRE

California Francophiles

When Richard and Kim Albarino asked for a garden inspired by the South of France, they envisioned a lived-in landscape with a "half-formal, half-ruined look," Richard explains. Landscape architect Katherine Spitz began by dividing their small Santa Monica front yard in half with a broad, straight walk. In the formal, geometric cutting plot (left and right), an update of the classic French parterre, straight lines enclose an exuberance of flowers chosen to bloom throughout the seasons: ranunculus and delphinium in spring, cosmos and larkspur in summer, cleomes and dahlias in fall. The other half of the garden, a spare, open field of decomposed granite, is accented with potted succulents. Spitz surrounded the two areas with a mix of Mediterranean and California native plants: French and Spanish lavender, rockrose, rosemary, westringia, echium, and ceanothus.

Bounded by Birch

An allée of white birch leads to the north wing of the Tudor Revival manor of Stan Hywet in Akron, Ohio, an estate created in the early years of the century by the cofounder of Goodyear Tire and Rubber Company. The landscaping of the estate, which has been open to the public since 1956, was planned by Warren H. Manning. The mansion and surrounding gardens were sited so that an axis drawn through the front and rear doors lines up with a fountain on the west terrace, a flight of steps leading to a cut in the woods, and a second terrace, where the view leads out to the woodlands. From the allée to the axial plan, the estate shows how ideas developed in France could be successfully adapted to American sites and plant materials.

An Arbor of Pears

It only takes a few well-placed trees to evoke the grandeur of the French allée. Visitors to Deborah Hornickel's Austin, Texas, garden (designed by James David) pass through a colorful area of annuals, perennials, and roses before entering the cool formality of the back garden. An allée edged with Bradford pear trees leads to a rock pedestal topped with a clay pot (right). The simple linear shapes formed by gravel paths and boxwood borders make the 60-by-180-foot lot seem much larger. Even the benches (left), one placed on each side of the allée, add to the geometric formality of the plan. Hornickel says that "lines, shapes, and forms" were her main priority, based on the advice of a friend who suggested she "work on the structure of your garden first."

Kitchen Gardens for Professionals

The rich alluvial soil of the Napa Valley supports the small, sophisticated garden of the French Laundry restaurant, where the potager is contained in seven 4-by-16-foot raised beds (right). Thomas Keller, winner of the 1997 James Beard Foundation's award for Best Chef in America, devotes four of the raised beds to lettuces and cooking greens, one and a half beds to herbs, and the rest to a constantly changing "chef's choice." The potager, he says, "gives the chefs a sense of seasonality. And because they grow the food themselves, they learn not to be wasteful." 'Merveille des Quatre Saisons', 'Brune d'Hiver', and 'Rouge d'Hiver' are among the lettuces grown in the raised beds; in the background is a cage for growing haricots verts.

In these garden plans, the vegetables, herbs, and edible flowers chosen by Thomas Keller and the chef-owners of two other restaurants with their own potagers—Greg and Mary Sonnier of Gabrielle in New Orleans and Craig Shelton of the Ryland Inn in Whitehouse, New Jersey—are arranged for the home garden.

Herb Garden

Keller's preferred herbs (right) range from delicately flavored winter savory to assertive tarragon and thymes. In each square of a 4-by-4-foot plot, plant two to four plants (grown in 2-inch pots). If you make substitutions, plant tall herbs in the center sections and low-growing ones around the outside.

1. Lemon thyme
2. Peppermint
3. Oregano
4. French thyme
5. Spearmint
6. Chives
7. Winter savory
8. Garlic chives
9. French tarragon
10. Rosemary
11. Sage
12. Sweet marjoram
13. 'Lime' thyme
14. Silver-leaved thyme

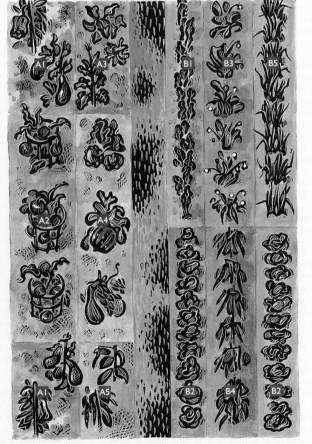

Vegetable Garden

Here are Shelton's picks for a 10-by-12-foot plot with a 2-foot-wide path (left). To get the most out of lettuces, harvest them young, warns sous-chef James Haurey. Replace each lettuce plant after two clippings, he says. For planting times and densities for the choices listed, check seed packets or nursery labels.

Bed A

A1 Eggplant 'Black Bell'; sweet red and sweet yellow peppers
A2 Tomatoes 'Brandywine', 'Red Pear', 'Yellow Pear'; 'Sweet Million' and yellow cherry tomatoes
A3 Cooking greens: sorrel, New Zealand spinach, red orach, tatsoi
A4 Yellow crookneck and zucchini summer squashes and/or cucumber 'Lemon'
A5 Beans 'Flambeau' and 'Maxibel' or potato 'Russian Banana'

Bed B

B1 Root vegetables: beets 'Golden' and 'Lutz Green Leaf'; carrot 'Minicor'
B2 Salad greens: claytonia; dandelion; mizuna; golden purslane; Good King Henry; lettuces 'Bibb', 'Buttercrunch', 'Curly Oakleaf', 'Lollo Rossa', 'Rosalita', 'Rossa d'Amerique', 'Royal Oakleaf'
B3 Fava bean 'Loreta'; after summer, replace with cabbage 'Columbia'
B4 Pea 'Sugarsnap'; after summer, replace with broccoli rabe
B5 Onions 'Purplette' and 'Snow Baby'

Container Garden

The Sonniers suggest placing a 3-foot Meyer lemon tree in a 30-inch pot (above). You can use the flowers and leaves of the tree as garnishes and the juice of its fruit to deglaze a pan. Around the tree, plant three 2-inch pots of each of two types of edible flowers and two kinds of herbs. The choices listed here thrive together.
A Edible flowers: nasturtiums, pansies, marigolds, violas
B Herbs: oregano, tarragon, marjoram, French thyme

Prolific Produce

Melons are made for abundance. Tender annuals that are native to Africa, the trailing vines are easy to grow—if you live in an area with hot, dry summers. In less torrid climates, gardeners trick the fruits by growing them on ground covered with black plastic mulch (top left), where the extra heat produces copious melons, like 'Queen Anne's Pockets' (bottom left). The gardener who grows melons can move beyond supermarket standbys like cantaloupe and honeydew, into a world whose broad variety is suggested by the melons grown by Amy P. Goldman in her garden in Rhinebeck, New York (right). Clockwise from top left: 'Bursa Turquie' melon; 'A Confire à Graine Verte' melon, partially obscuring an unripe 'Early Black Rock' melon; 'Legacy' watermelon; 'Moon and Stars' watermelon; 'Banana' melon; 'Cob' melon; ripe (cut) 'Early Black Rock'; 'Jelly' melon; and 'Vert Grimpant' melon.

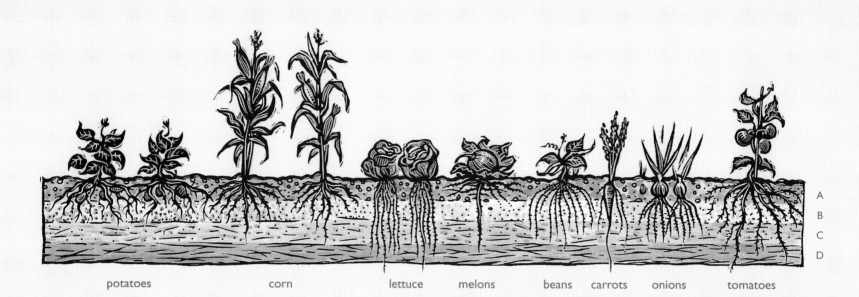

potatoes   corn   lettuce   melons   beans   carrots   onions   tomatoes

A
B
C
D

Intensive Care

In a "lazy bed" (above), designed by John Jeavons, crops are arranged so that deep-rooted and shallow-rooted plants complement one another. Vegetables can be planted closer than normal (the stylized sketch greatly simplifies the number of plants), because double digging has improved the soil. The raised bed is built of (A) compost and topsoil, (B) enriched and loosened soil, (C) partially enriched subsoil, and (D) subsoil.

Biodynamic Beds

Through a process known as "biodynamic" gardening, advocate John Jeavons has turned a small plot into a cornucopia that can produce yields two to six times that of conventional agriculture. The biodynamic method uses deep digging, close planting, regular composting, no chemical fertilizers or pesticides, and, like the old *jardin de curé*, companion planting to increase yields. "It's something you can do in your own backyard. It's good exercise, it's beautiful, and you can design an action solution to global problems," says Jeavons, who practices what he preaches at Ecology Action in Willits, California. A staked square of 'Golden Giant' amaranth (left) produces nutritious grain as well as carbonaceous material for the compost. Neighbors include alfalfa, garlic, and cardoon. Compact planting (opposite bottom) ensures that growing leaves will touch, forming a living mulch.

ABUNDANCE: VERTICAL GROWTH

Creative Heights

Susan Mikula's plot in the Northampton, Massachusetts, Community Gardens (left) uses an imaginative rustic fence to create height and boundaries. "I wanted both strong shapes and romantic abundance," she says, "a kind of tricked-out kitchen garden that also afforded the comfort of good geometry." 'Kentucky Wonder' and 'Yellow Annelino' beans scale tepees, while 'Grandpa Ott's' morning glories and sunflowers climb the fence, which was designed by local artisan Michael Poole.

Up Against a Wall

Following a centuries-old technique to espalier apples against the side of a barn (right), Renny Reynolds and Jack Staub added both height and decorative effect to the large vegetable garden on their 72-acre farm in Bucks County, Pennsylvania. Other vertical elements in their garden include trellises for growing tomatoes, wire-screened tepees to keep rabbits out of the greens, and a formal metal tuteur for twining pole beans.

FRAGRANCE: SCENT GARDEN

Uncommon Scents

"What distinguishes many of my garden designs is the subtle use of fragrant plants," says landscape architect Stephen Suzman, who turned an unattractive backyard in the Eureka Valley neighborhood of San Francisco into a lush, aromatic garden (right). Among the flowers that perfume the air are *Magnolia grandiflora* (left); *Clematis armandii*; the classic climbing rose 'Cécile Brünner'; star jasmine; wild ginger; and *Clethra arborea*, the fragrant Lily-of-the-valley tree that is a native of Madeira and scents the air with vanilla. Also releasing their perfumes into the garden are *Daphne odora; Rhododendron fragariiflorum* 'Fragrantissimum'; Angel's-trumpet *(Brugmansia suaveolens)*; a variety of herbs and pelargoniums; heliotrope; *Nicotiana sylvestris*; the roses 'Agnes', 'Medallion', and 'Royal Sunset'; *Buddleia davidii; Wisteria sinensis*; and the Golden-chain tree, *Laburnum* x *watereri* 'Vossii'.

Fun and Function

Nowhere is it written that garden furniture must be made of stone or wood—or that pieces can't serve equally well indoors and outdoors. A graceful and whimsical wrought-iron French sofa from the 1930s (left) warms up a shady corner of the garden, where wisteria adorns an arbor. The permanent—and practical—vinyl cushions are given a party cover-up with colorful fabrics by Boussac.

Instant Attitude

"Old says instant maturity," declares Robert Ziesmer, a dealer in garden antiques in Danville, Kentucky, who is known for the gently mottled surfaces of the pots, sculpture, sundials, fountains, and furniture he sells. "There's nothing like an urn covered in lichens to give a brand-new flower bed a mellowed quality." Among the most popular collectibles in the recent mania for vintage outdoor accessories are florid, curly metal pieces like the French balloon-back armchairs (right) Ziesmer discovered in Nashville.

Decorative Detail

What someone called "ephemera with attitude" has been turning up in the garden for centuries. Sometimes it was by accident, as when a trowel got lost in a tangle of dirt and vines and showed up years later covered with rust and character. Sometimes it was for a practical purpose: an elaborate mobile clattering in the breeze to scare off predators. Now gardeners are learning that antique ornaments, like a rust-softened late-19th-century gate from Ohio (left), can enhance the garden.

Vintage Vignette

An antique French wrought-iron table (right) in a trellised entryway acts as a pedestal for a glazed yellow pot, its mustard tones setting off the purple of the violas. The curvaceous quality of the table helps it to stand out against the dramatic backdrop of the contrasting foliage and heights of baptisia, phlox, *Weigela florida*, and variegated red twig dogwood.

201

garden
TOUR

A pair of gates swings open on a wide, gravel allée, which leads through an arbor dripping honeysuckle and past a quadrant of rectangles edged in boxwood, drawing the eye across a large expanse of lawn before stopping at a wall where a mirrored porthole feeds the image back—a classic optical illusion. Someone has been reading Dézallier d'Argenville's 1709 treatise on creating a formal garden. Or have they? The stately measures that set the French marching through their formal gardens have taken on a different beat as they've moved around the world.

The Long Island garden created by art critic and writer Robert Hughes, born and educated in Australia, and his ex-wife, Victoria, a California native, demonstrates that French ideas can indeed be imported to America—if they are properly adapted. The garden has parterres and allées, along with the obligatory cross-axis, a fountain, and boxwood topiary spiraling (continued on page 206)

RELAXED FORMALITY Boxwood hedges in the parterre contain the hot colors of *Berberis thunbergii* 'Crimson Pygmy' and red-hot-pokers. *Lonicera periclymenum* 'Graham Thomas' covers the arbor, which arches over a gravel path following the main axis.

Colorful Contrast

Instead of replicating the classical parterre, in which patterns are made from single plants in single colors or from colored gravel or sand, the Hugheses chose to use a variety of plantings and strong colors to contrast with the dark walls of the house. A cone of boxwood (left) anchors *Potentilla fruticosa* 'Primrose Beauty', *Allium schubertii*, and *Amsonia ciliata*. Beyond the formal garden is a potager where Robert Hughes experiments with vegetables— white eggplants, hot peppers, new varieties of lettuce, all grown from seed—as well as an orchard with apricot, peach, pear, and apple trees.

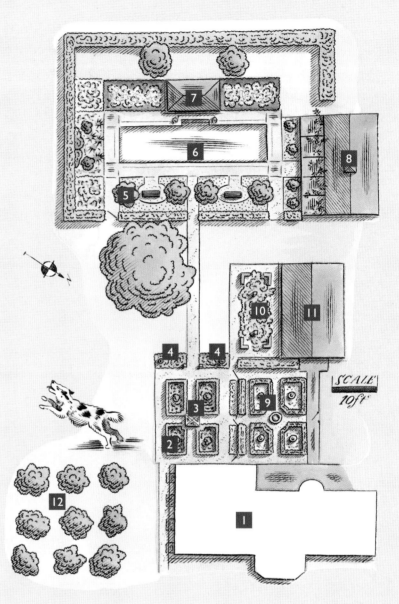

Garden Plan

A path draws the main axis linking the house and the pool. The vegetable garden and potting shed are out of sight to the south.

1. House
2. Yellow parterre
3. Arbor
4. Dry garden
5. Pool garden
6. Pool
7. Pool house
8. Guesthouse
9. Courtyard garden
10. Rose garden
11. Carpentry barn
12. Orchard

(continued from page 202) from containers around a reflecting *miroir d'eau*. But the French formality, translated to American soil, with a breeze from Australia blowing through, has become as much a child of the 20th century as Le Nôtre's linear landscape was of the 17th.

In the Hughes garden, the parterres are filled with an array of plants in eye-catching colors that Louis XIV's gardener would never have allowed. Too varied for the simple demands of geometry, too hot for the cool rationality of the age of Descartes, these quadrants vibrate with the life and color of *Berberis thunbergii* 'Crimson Pygmy' and red-hot-pokers. The hot colors often favored in climates where the sun bleaches pastels—places like Australia and California—are used in the cooler climate of Long Island because they help offset the dark, shingled walls of the Hugheses' Victorian farmhouse.

And as for the miroir d'eau, it is only a still plane of water reflecting the sky and clouds when it isn't being churned up by the owners, who use it as a lap pool. The pool garden, which is enclosed by a hedge, has complex planting on one side, a mix of shrubs, perennials, annuals, and bulbs in soft shades of silver, mauve, and blue. The other side is given over to a single, huge sheet of *Liriope spicata*, a rampant grower that, when put in a more varied bed, is likely to fight with its neighbors. With no other plants to push around, the ground cover has been turned into an imaginative lawn, long enough to shimmer in the shifts of light and shade.

Despite the reflection of passing clouds in the pool and the movement of the lilylike leaves, the Hugheses were concerned that the garden looked too static. Victoria Hughes and Jeff Mendoza, the garden designer who had helped them tie their landscape together, decided to lighten the formality by cutting the top of the surrounding hedge into waves. "Inserting whimsy into a formal space brought the garden alive," says Mendoza.

And planted the formal French landscape firmly onto American ground.

GEOMETRY WITH A TWIST
The pool garden's wavy hedge dips and rises behind a row of *Magnolia stellata* and a "lawn" of the rampant grower *Liriope spicata*, dotted with pots of succulents. The geometry of the landscape is continued in the blocks of bluestone paving that surround the pool, the gridwork on the wooden gate, and the trio of ovals on the back of the bench.

the
TROPICS

With but few and unimportant exceptions a great forest band from a thousand to fif-teen hundred miles in width girdles the earth at the equator, clothing hill, plain, and mountain with an evergreen mantle," wrote the Welsh naturalist Alfred Russel Wallace in 1891, describing the tropical regions where he spent many years of his life. "Often the woody covering continues to a height of eight or ten thousand feet, as in some of the volcanic mountains of Java and on portions of the Eastern Andes." Although there are arid regions in the tropics, it is that great green mantle that most people associate with the area between the tropic of Cancer and the tropic of Capricorn—a damp, exuberant Eden, where things grow with a quickness beyond a gardener's wildest dreams. ■ But the very richness of the tropics makes it difficult to write about the region's gardens. Nature's fertile reach is not held in check by the boundaries of a man-made plot. "The land is one great wild, untidy, luxuriant hothouse, made by Nature for herself, but taken possession of by man," wrote Charles Darwin of a shore visit to Bahia on the coast of Brazil. To maintain that possession, the tropical gardener must work with a spade in one hand and a machete in the other. ■ It is difficult to find descriptions of any ornamental gardens in the tropics before the arrival of outsiders who came to explore or to conquer. The Spaniards left reports of extraordinary gardens made by the Incas, and of flowers growing among food crops on the floating gar-dens of the Aztecs. These floating gardens, called *chinampas*, were built out of roots and reeds, covered with 3 to 4 feet of rich lake mud, and joined together to make large rafts. The chinampas increased the amount of land available for planting, and because the lakes weren't deep, gardeners could pole the rafts to market. Visitors must have found them an extraordinary sight, these floating fields full of vegetables and flowers. ■ For men

interested in making a fortune, as well as for horticulturists fascinated by the new plants, the tropics offered endless opportunities. In the 18th century botanical gardens were set up in St. Vincent in the West Indies, in Jamaica, Calcutta, and Penang to experiment with plants that might have commercial value—as indeed many, like rubber and coffee, did. In the 19th century new gardens were established in Rio de Janeiro, Buenos Aires, and Caracas as more people took interest in what the tropics might hold. They titillated themselves with tales of the man-eating tree of Madagascar, yearned for the brilliant pelargonium and the vivid nasturtium, and, if they could afford it, added glasshouses to provide the proper environment for the tropical flora. ■ For some time, gardeners in temperate regions had been using what they called stove houses to provide warmth for tender plants, but these were expensive and labor-intensive affairs heated first with open fires, then with enclosed Dutch stoves. The 1845 repeal of the glass tax and the discovery that heat could be obtained by circulating hot water through pipes made greenhouses affordable to the middle class, while the construction in 1851 of the Crystal Palace in Hyde Park created a craze for conservatories to hold the exotic flora of the tropics. ■ It is an enthusiasm that persists today as people create tropical jungles in living rooms or greenhouses. But it is also a mania that may consume what it seeks. Development is laying waste to the tropical forests. Some plants face extinction because they're losing their habitat; others are at risk because collectors, profiting from the high prices that rarities bring, are tearing them out of the wild. Early European travelers to the tropics thought they had landed in Eden—a garden destroyed by greed. It would be tragic if today's gardeners, in the name of loving plants, helped destroy Darwin's "great wild, untidy, luxuriant hothouse."

elements of **tropical** garden style

epiphyte A plant that grows fixed to the bark or branches of a tree but, unlike mistletoe and other parasites, does not steal nourishment from its host. Among these tree-perching flora (sometimes called air plants) are orchids, bromeliads, ferns, and even some tropical cacti.

tropics Includes the entire region lying between the tropic of Cancer and the tropic of Capricorn—temperate areas and arid deserts as well as mountainous regions and rain forests. For gardening purposes, tropical and subtropical plants are those that need a climate where the temperature ranges from a low of 60° to a high of 86°.

canteiros Of Roman origin, these plant beds or stone boxes that seem to float in the middle of pools were used in Portugal through the 18th century. (The Aztecs used similar beds, though theirs actually floated.) Ideal for tropical settings, they were adapted by Brazilian landscape designer Roberto Burle Marx for his contemporary garden designs (as in the Clemente Gomes garden near Areias, Brazil, opposite).

understory Much of the dense lushness of the tropical forest is due to the way nature makes use of space. The understory is composed of plants that grow under trees, benefiting from the shade provided by the leafy canopy overhead. Understory plants, in turn, serve as a living mulch, adding their leaves to the forest floor.

nurse plants Plants that help other plants grow—whether by providing the proper environment for germination or a tree trunk to climb to reach the light. Most cacti seedlings shelter beneath a nurse plant, usually a tree or shrub, to avoid the consequences of a long drought or a sudden drop in temperature.

xerophyte A plant that has adapted to an arid climate by reducing its water loss. Some grasses accomplish this with rolled leaves that shield them from the sun. In cacti, leaves are eliminated altogether, spines provide shade, and water is stored in a succulent stem, which is covered with a waxy skin that reduces surface evaporation.

a spirit of exuberance

Gauguin's Tahitian paintings show the shock of color that must have stunned every traveler who sailed away from the soft pastels of the temperate world and entered the brilliance of the tropics.

Writers searched for the imagery to describe nature's overpowering and vivid presence. Charles Darwin wrote: "Who when examining in the cabinet of the entomologist the gay exotic butterflies, and singular cicadas, will associate with these lifeless objects, the ceaseless harsh music of the latter, and the lazy flight of the former—the sure accompaniments of the still, glowing noonday of the tropics?"

Unable to re-create the tangled jungle where nature lives on fast-forward, 19th-century gardeners did the best they could by opening their conservatories to the exotic plants sent back by explorers. More than 200,000 species flourish in the tropics, and though only a small fraction were shipped back to the temperate zone, gardeners were delighted by the colors and stunned by the size of the tropical imports.

Victorians read Sir Joseph Paxton's account of how he brought the world's largest water lily, the South American *Victoria amazonica*, into flower. Aldous Huxley, who was in Southeast Asia in the 1920s, wrote of "lilies in Malaya whose petals have become attenuated to writhing tentacles, so that they dangle on their stalks like perfumed spiders."

The sinuous shapes and intense colors add one more vibration to air alive with the swaying of leaf and vine, the flight of insects and birds, the flurry of flora growing, dying, and falling to the ground to become the soil in which new things grow—a world where life is never at rest.

TROPICAL BRUSH
Landscape designer Made Wijaya laid out his Villa Bebek in Bali as a traditional walled compound of thatched pavilions with shaded verandas opening onto courtyards. One courtyard (above) features a pool surrounded by lush tropical plants. Opposite: Bombax, *Pseudobombax ellipticum,* is also known as shaving brush tree. A Central American native, it blooms in the spring.

VIVID ENVIRONS
Architect Luis Barragán drew on his travels in North Africa and Europe to create vibrant structures and gardens filled with light and color in his native Mexico. The back garden of the Gálvez House (this page) in Chimalistac is enlivened by his signature colored walls. Opposite: Brazilian landscape architect Roberto Burle Marx designed the sidewalks of boldly patterned mosaics that run along the three-mile-long Copacabana beachfront in Rio de Janeiro.

PARADISE FOUND

In 1924 French painter Jacques Majorelle created La Majorelle Gardens in Marrakech, Morocco, as a studio and a retreat. He tinted his walls a startling shade of azure that became known as—what else?—Majorelle blue. After his death in 1962 the property was abandoned, until designer Yves Saint Laurent restored it. Now visitors can stroll amid coconut palms, bananas, and bougainvillea, and visit a museum of Islamic art housed in the converted studio.

plants as sculpture

When the Spaniards made their way to Yucay in Peru, they found that the Incas had planted "parterres...glowing with the various forms of vegetable life skilfully imitated in gold and silver!" Among these, William H. Prescott wrote in his *History of the Conquest of Mexico and History of the Conquest of Peru*, was Indian corn: "The curious workmanship is noticed with which the golden ear was half disclosed amidst the broad leaves of silver, and the light tassel of the same material that floated gracefully from its top."

Today we're so used to stately stalks of corn that it takes more unusual objects to catch our eye—the narrow arching leaves of the bromeliad, the rotund and portly barrel cactus. In spring the Santa Rita prickly pear (*Opuntia violacea* var. *macrocentra*) sets a halo of yellow flowers on the edges of its flat, violet pads, while the rare cycad *Encephalartos gratus*, a native of tropical Africa, looks like a green feather duster trying to climb out of a bulbous brown vase.

It is easier to see the form of the cactus, outlined against the desert floor, than to distinguish a single tree in a tropical forest; but Herman Melville found sculpture in the leaves of the breadfruit tree, whose "edges are cut and scalloped as fantastically as those of a lady's lace collar." The fruit, he wrote, was "dotted all over with little conical prominences looking not unlike the knobs on an antiquated church door."

Whether it is the rayed face of the sunflower, worshipped by the Incas as a living image of the Sun God, or a pineapple finial perched on a post, when gardeners take time to look, all plants become art.

FANTASTIC FORMS
The clump-forming heliconia (above), a relative of the banana, has long-stalked, paddle-shaped leaves and produces fiery red bracts. Outside the tropics, it is best grown in a conservatory or greenhouse. Opposite: The striking shapes of agaves (like the *Agave neo-mexicana*) punctuate the arid landscapes of Central America, Mexico, and the southwestern United States.

HISTORICAL THAI
Prasart Vongsakul has housed both an art museum and a 25-acre garden in a suburban area outside Bangkok. The garden, which combines historical Thai elements with modern-day tropical horticulture, includes a collection of palms representing about 60 species. Lotus (this page), a staple of Bangkok water gardens, is a customary offering at Buddhist rites in Thailand. Opposite: The Thai version of topiary is believed to have been borrowed from the Chinese in the 13th or 14th century, when Sukhothai, north of Bangkok, was the capital of Siam.

225

conserving native flora

In an introduction to the 1996 book *Wild Cactus*, ethnobotanist Gary Paul Nabhan wrote: "All the potted plantings in the world cannot save a species from ecological extinction—that is, the extinction of its natural relationships with pollinators, seed dispersers, root fungi, and nurse plants."

The interdependence of living things is illustrated not only by the relationships that help a plant to survive, but also by those that keep it in check and prevent it from overwhelming its neighbors. The water hyacinth (*Eichhornia crassipes*), a native of South America, has naturalized throughout the tropics and subtropics. When brought to Louisiana toward the end of the 19th century, it grew rampant, uncontrolled by predators or climate; it so clogged the rivers and streams that someone wrote to a newspaper suggesting that the hippopotamus be introduced to eat it, as that animal does in Africa.

But if a weed is any plant growing where it's not wanted, a bad plant is simply one that's been snatched out of its natural environment. Even the water hyacinth is of value to more than a hungry hippo; its ability to absorb pollutants through its roots has led some water treatment plants to use it to purify water.

Nature loses its balance when a plant is taken from its home, or when the home is taken from the plant, as happens when the rain forest is clear-cut or the desert is covered with housing subdivisions. Separated from its environment, almost any good plant may turn bad. Or it may simply vanish altogether.

PROTECTING CACTI
Known as a barrel cactus, *Echinocactus platyacanthus* (above) usually grows 3 to 4 feet tall. In the mid-19th century, however, a 713-pound example was collected in Mexico for the Royal Botanic Gardens at Kew. Opposite: The conservatory at Cante, a botanical garden in San Miguel de Allende, Mexico, houses more than 2,000 plant species.

the **conservation** gracener

By 1620 the Bermuda Assembly had passed "An Act Agaynst The Killinge of Ouer Yonge Tortoyses," because green turtles were being taken in dangerously large numbers by "sundrye lewd and impvident psons inhabitinge within these Islands."

This early attempt at legislating conservation failed, but it shows that even then, when explorers were discovering new worlds that seemed infinitely rich in resources, there were those who understood the connections of nature. Cut the teak, pluck the orchids, clear the rain forest, or irrigate the desert, and all things around will change. The plants that grew there will die and the creatures that ate them will vanish.

Over time, more people have become aware of the way nature spins its web, and this consciousness has produced a new kind of gardener: the conservationist, who wants a beautiful garden but also wants to preserve plants. Roberto Burle Marx was a conservation gardener,

gathering 3,500 species of tropical flora on his estate outside Rio de Janeiro. So is Jonathan Surtees (left), the plantsman-in-residence at the Strawberry Hill resort in Jamaica's Blue Mountains, where a tour of the gardens is a botanical stroll through the vegetation of all Jamaica.

The late Charlie Glass, a cactus specialist, was also a conservation gardener. He established the conservatory at Cante in San Miguel de Allende, Mexico, in 1991, eventually building the world's largest collection of Mexican cacti and succulents. Central to his process was going into the wild with his staff to catalog and collect endangered plants, which they then propagated. When a dam in Nayarit caused waters to rise, the group set out in boats to rescue endangered flora. Despite being attacked by killer bees while traversing water awash with crocodiles, they saved 7,000 specimens.

And some gardeners complain about midges, mosquitoes, and moles!

TROPICAL RESORT
Trails snake through a dense landscape of costus and 200-year-old juniper at Strawberry Hill (this page), a resort in the Blue Mountains of Jamaica. The 6-acre grounds were laid out by Hawaiian landscape architect Stephen Haus in a fashion that leads plantsman-in-residence Jonathan Surtees (opposite) to say, "The best tropical gardens aren't meant to be taken in at a glance. They should be *discovered*." Using material collected from an earlier botanical garden on the plantation, as well as imported tropical plants, Surtees and his staff of six have developed "an island of rare specimens, hoping to make them common."

adapting to the habitat

In those areas between the tropic of Capricorn and the tropic of Cancer where the rains rarely fall and the earth seems a dry, barren place, a closer look reveals a lively network of plants and creatures that have adapted to their desert habitat—and to each other. The cactus is a xerophyte, capable of surviving in an area of high temperatures and low rainfall by doing away with the extravagance of leaves and storing water in its succulent stem. Desert animals eat the cactus: some learn to dine between the spines; others, like the javelina, have evolved kidneys that excrete the cactus's poisonous oxalic acid. Birds nest in the branches, insects feed on the plants, and the cacti themselves may depend on "nurse plants" to provide the shelter they need to germinate and grow.

And in the wet and fertile forests, woody creepers and climbers wind themselves around the trunks of taller trees. "They drop down pendant from the branches, they stretch tightly from tree to tree, they hang looped in huge festoons from bough to bough, they twist in great serpentine coils or lie in entangled masses on the ground," wrote the 19th-century naturalist Alfred Russel Wallace. Vines need both the rich decay of the jungle floor and the height of the tree to reach the light.

The forest is full of such partnerships: Bromeliads and epiphytic cacti grow in the forks of trees, though they don't hurt their hosts. Other plants grow in the understory, because they need the forest's protective canopy to live. Animals, insects, plants, people—no single element inhabiting the tropics is self-sufficient; everything is helping something else survive.

CACTUS AND FERN
A living museum of tropical flora covers the Brazilian estate of the late Roberto Burle Marx (above). An epiphytic cactus dangles down between staghorn ferns; in front are native *Anthurium coriaceum*. Opposite: Layered in levels of understory and overstory, tropical plants create a lush setting in the entry garden of the famed Amandari resort on Bali.

LAYERED GROUNDS
Hacienda Katanchel, a resort near Mérida, was created on an estate that had been a henequen (*Agave fourcroydes*) plantation, which covered the site of a colonial Spanish cattle ranch, which, in turn, had been laid out on the ruins of a Mayan settlement. All the gardens, including a token planting of henequen (this page) and the lush courtyard of a guest cottage (opposite), benefit from underground rivers and sinkholes. The system of crop rotation in the kitchen gardens—where the fast-growing leaves of lettuces shade the delicate shoots of peppers—makes the best of the intense Yucatán sun.

bringing it
HOME

There are few places in the United States where tropical plants will survive the winter, but that hasn't stopped gardeners from creating their own versions of the tropics. Using brilliant colors and thick plantings, gardeners have found that if you build it, they will come—they being the birds, insects, and wildlife that take shelter in the dense foliage. It may be a goldfinch instead of a parrot, a frog and not an iguana, but gardens planted with a thick cover serve as sanctuary in the temperate zone just as they do in the tropics. Gardeners in arid areas appreciate the cactus for its sculptural shape, its short-lived but spectacular flowers, and its conservation of water. In colder climates, tropical plants may be treated as annuals, while succulents can be moved into the garden in the spring and returned to the living room or greenhouse when winter threatens. By paying attention to habitat and putting plants where they want to be, American gardeners have found that any temperate garden can have a tropical hue.

Thriving on the Trade Winds

Writer and artist May Moir's garden, Lipolani ("tropical heaven"), in the Nuuanu Valley above Honolulu, is a mass of dense vegetation pierced by the brilliant colors of orchids and the boldly marked foliage and sculptural shapes of bromeliads. When the vanda beetle arrived in Hawaii in the 1960s and destroyed many of the orchids in the garden (Moir's late husband, W. W. Goodale Moir, an agronomist, wrote four books on orchids), the Moirs planted bromeliads in their place, some of which were started from seeds collected on their travels. To enclose the northeast-facing garden, Moir used hollow concrete blocks instead of a solid wall, because, she explains, "The trade winds blowing through the walls supply a perfect environment for the bromeliads to thrive."

235

Annual Jungle

On a rooftop overlooking Philadelphia's Old City (left), florist Matthew Drozd Jr. has created a miniature jungle of exotic annuals. Among the plants he favors are *Aristolochia gigantea*, the scarlet Amaranthus tricolor (*Amaranthus gangeticus*), and the yellow and white lollipop flower (*Pachystachys lutea*), which, according to Drozd, "blooms perpetually until the cold weather comes."

Temperate Tropics

Influenced by his travels in Southeast Asia and India, Jeffrey Bale brings the tropics to his garden (right) in temperate Portland, Oregon, by re-creating the lushness and abundance of steamier climes. Clockwise from top left: Pots of herbs make a junglelike thicket at the door; a bed hung with Asian temple bells is set near a pond surrounded by rhododendron and white *Geranium* x *magnificum* and sheltered under *Mahonia lomariifolia;* Bale rests in a doorway; dahlias float in a bowl flanked by lacecap hydrangea, *Hakonechloa macra* 'Aureola', sedum, and Labrador violets.

237

EXUBERANCE: DENSE GROWTH

L.A. Luxuriance

When Jay Griffith and Rob Steiner designed this Los Angeles pool, they avoided the usual hard-scaped deck, which sets a pool off from the garden and makes it look sterile and utilitarian. Instead, they created the feel of a tropical waterway by siting the pool under overhanging trees and sur-rounding it with abundant and imaginative plantings. The litter of fallen leaves, which makes many pool owners forgo the plea-sures of shade and the shifting reflections of branch and leaf, is mini-mized by an automatic pool cover. Near the pool, lamb's ears, fortnight lilies, and ground morn-ing glories can survive the harsh conditions caused by foot traffic and chlo-rine. Griffith and Steiner saved tender plants like *Rosa* 'Iceberg', *R.* 'La Reine', *R.* 'Intrigue', and *R.* 'Simplicity' for spots farther from the pool.

THE PLANT LIST
Everything growing poolside is as tough as nails. Sited a bit farther from the water's edge, roses are thriving, but Griffith and Steiner warn that tender plants are a risky proposition within splashing range of chlorine.
1. Fern pine (*Podocarpus gracilior*) 2. Tree fern (*Dicksonia*)
3. Weeping bottle brush (*Callistemon viminalis*) 4. Fort-night lily (*Dietes bicolor*) 5. Ground morning glory (*Convolvulus mauritanicus*) 6. *Artemisia* 'Powis Castle'
7. *Lavandula latifolia* 8. *Stachys lanata* 9. Australian tree fern (*Sphaeropteris cooperi*) 10. Japanese aralia (*Fatsia japonica*) 11. Meadow rue (*Thalictrum delavayi* 'Hewitts Double') 12. *Geranium incanum* 13. Walnut (*Juglans californica*) 14. *Santolina rosmarinifolia ssp. rosmarinifolia*
15. *Lavandula dentata* 16. Siberian iris 17. *Rosmarinus prostratus* 18. *Rosa* 'Iceberg' 19. *Salvia patens* 20. *Thymus pseudolanuginosus* 21. *Salvia chamaedryoides* 22. *Rosa* 'La Reine' 23. *Rosa* 'Intrigue' 24. *Rosa* 'Simplicity'
25. *Santolina chamaecyparissus* 26. Brazilian pepper tree (*Schinus terebinthifolius*) 27. *Pittosporum tobira* 'Variegatum'

Prickly Pair

When Judy and Sidney Zuber commissioned architect Antoine Predock to design their starkly modern, sculptural house near Phoenix, Arizona, they also hired landscape designer Nancy Wagner to provide an appropriate setting. She responded with a design featuring low-maintenance native plants. "We didn't want to detract from the architecture with busy plantings," she says. Outside the door is a sculptural array of golden barrel cacti, Peruvian cereus, agave, and yucca. An ocotillo (*Fouquieria splendens*) (left) makes a stark diagonal line against the geometry of the house. The yellow flowers of the Santa Rita prickly pear cactus (*Opuntia violacea* var. *macrocentra*) (right) bloom abundantly from April through June.

SCULPTURE: BOLD FORMS

Flamboyant Flora

"Gardening is about proportion, color, texture," says Suzanne Lipschutz, who lives and gardens in Miami Beach. "Low and high, circles and squares." Like the furniture and objects Lipschutz sells in her New York store, Secondhand Rose, the plants she favors in her zone 10 garden are visually flamboyant. "I'm amazed by tropical plants," she says. One of the more striking sights in her garden is pinecone ginger (*Zingiber spectabile*) (left), a native of Malaysia that can reach 6 feet or more in height. An ornamental rather than edible ginger, it can be grown in a greenhouse with a minimum temperature of 60°. Lipschutz also grows *Datura metel* 'Flore Pleno' (right), a tender annual from India that is as hallucinogenic as it looks.

243

Just Deserts

Begun as a cactus garden in 1905 and later expanded to include other xerophytes, the 12-acre desert garden at the Huntington Botanical Gardens in San Marino, California, now contains more than 5,000 species. Many of the plants are organized in beds that represent flora from Baja California, various South American regions, the Canary Islands, Madagascar, and other areas. Growing in front of the cactuses *Cereus dayami* and *Cereus peruvianus (C. Uruguayanus)* (left) is the succulent *Senecio mandraliscae*; looming in the background is the Mexican fan palm, *Washingtonia robusta,* which usually grows in desert oases. The bright pink flowers of Lampranthus and the red blossoms of *Aloe arborescens* (right) demonstrate the beauty of desert plants in bloom.

Indoor Beauties

Given conditions that approximate their natural habitat, orchids can overcome their reputation as hothouse weaklings to become robust indoor plants. The leaves of *Phragmipedium* Grande 'Macrochilum', AM/AOS (the initials indicate an award from the American Orchid Society), arch away from the 5-foot flower spikes (left). Native to the stream banks of Central and South America, they thrive on dampness but should be allowed to dry out when they've stopped blooming. Cirrhopetalums, creeping plants native to tropical rain forests, grow well in shallow pots with plenty of water. A plant like the spectacular *Cirrhopetalum* Elizabeth Ann 'Buckleberry', FCC/AOS (right), will feel at home if it is given warmth and humidity and kept in an area with low light.

247

Succulent Garden

On an acre of coastline north of San Francisco, landscape architect Isis Spinola-Schwartz and designer-ecologist David Schwartz have created a lush sanctuary overlooking rugged cliffs and churning surf. Isis drew on her memories of the extravagant vegetation of Brazil, where she grew up. David inherited his obsession with succulents (which thrive with little water and can tolerate the salt spray) from his father, who often took him on collecting trips to Mexico and Africa. Dead man's fingers, *Dudleya linearis* (*Cotyledon linearis*) (left), bloom under a handrail of driftwood found on the beach, and *Aloe striata* flowers near wild strawberries and lamb's ears. Ground-hugging gray echeveria and rosy *Dudleya linearis* (top right) are native to Mexico and the south-western United States; *Cotyledon orbiculata* (bottom right) is native to South Africa.

Reading Her Palms

When she began garden-
ing in Miami Beach,
Suzanne Lipschutz (left), a
transplanted New York,
had to adapt to her new
surroundings. "The whole
idea of cutting back is
alien to anyone who gar-
dens up north," she says. "I
used to dust delphiniums.
Nurture sticks. Now I
garden with a machete."
Lipschutz, who says
she didn't know a thing
about tropical gardening,
learned from Hurricane
Andrew. "He ripped off
the plant canopy here.
Everything underneath
was fine for a while, and
then it burned up—in-
stant death. That's when I
understood that gardening
down here is about shade.
These layers of plants are
interdependent. They
can't survive without
one another." Illustrating
her point, Lipschutz
uses a screw palm (right)
as a home for a pair of
bromeliads.

ADAPTING: NATIVE PLANTS

At Home in Florida

In Pan's Garden (left), in Palm Beach, Florida, a 150-by-250-foot lot has become a showcase for native plants. Begun by the city's Preservation Foundation in 1993 and opened to the public the following year, the garden contains plants that are indigenous not just to Florida but to the Palm Beach area in particular. Landscape architects Jorge Sanchez and Phil Maddux spent a year studying the region's history, going as far back as Native American cultures, before obtaining plants and laying out the garden.

At Home in California

When Henry Valdez (right) tended other people's gardens, he was appalled at the water that was wasted maintaining plants not suited to the Los Angeles area. After he and his family moved to Inglewood, his first act was to get rid of the grass in front of his house and plant cholla, echinocactus, and palo verde—plants that can survive on a minimum of water. "It's always green here," he says, "because these plants never change except when they're in bloom."

garden
TOUR

Leland Miyano has transformed an acre of land at Kahalu'u, at the foot of the Ko'olau Mountains on the windward 'Oahu, into a garden that is as botanically interesting as it is beautiful. A painter and sculptor as well as a gardener, Miyano has been evolving with the garden since his family acquired the property in the 1970s while he was a student at the University of Hawaii in Honolulu. It was a modest plot of land, and practical, with a level and stoneless terrain. Leland's sister made a volleyball court; his father raised rabbits; Leland mowed the lawn.

Mowing grass will put any youngster firmly on the side of letting nature do its thing, but Miyano gained this wisdom in a different way. He was the kind of child who kept his eyes to the ground, finding things and, naturally, wanting to bring them home. One of these found objects—a large-shelled African snail—taught him a lesson that has shaped his garden *(continued on page 258)*

HAWAIIAN MAZE
Leland Miyano laid the basalt pathways that wind through the garden by following rainwater runoff channels. In the garden's lava- and humus-filled soil, Miyano has planted a wide range of native and non-native species, growing Hawaiian *Wikstroemia uva-ursi* and *Pritchardia martii*, for instance, near South American *Philodendron adamantinum*.

Jungle Creatures

Koko the dog perches in a *Dracaena marginata*, as at home on his jungle roost as a macaw or a monkey. The *Dracaena* is a host tree for epiphytes, plants that grow on other plants but don't use them as a source of nutrition.

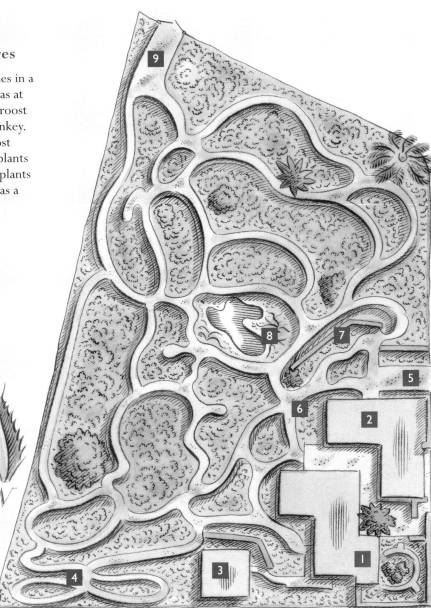

Garden Plan

1. House
2. Studio and garage
3. Pavilion
4. Rain forest area
5. Main entry
6. Cut basalt paths
7. Freestanding wall
8. Pond
9. Driveway

(continued from page 254) as surely as has his artist's view. An import into the islands, the African snail was not a good guest, and the damage it caused led the Hawaii Department of Agriculture to try to eradicate it. Deciding to set a thief to catch a thief, they imported other carnivorous snails. But rather than attacking the African snails, the newer imports devoured the beautiful and harmless Hawaiian land snails. At the end of this extended meal, hundreds of species of snails that existed nowhere else were on the verge of extinction, or were already extinct.

The African snail taught Miyano that interfering with nature, even when we mean to help, can have unexpected effects. When he contemplates his garden, he reminds himself that however much we may think we know, ignorance is always with us. Miyano eventually bought the family home from his parents and began to plant a garden. He found that he had a rich pocket of soil, fed with lava and humus from the erosion of the Ko'olau Mountains. He cut weed trees like the mango and Java plum and planted cycads in island beds, where they grew larger and larger. He made winding paths of basalt, following rainwater runoff channels. And he continued to read about plants and gardens, as well as fossils and life-forms of different kinds and habitats.

After meeting Roberto Burle Marx, Miyano made several trips to Brazil, spending time with the great landscape architect and accompanying him on travels to the Atlantic coastal rain forest and to other regions of Brazil, where they rescued endangered plants, explored, and visited gardens. The influence of Burle Marx, who had created his own collection of native plants on his estate near Rio de Janeiro, shaped Miyano's view of the role of the gardener in the natural world as much as did that long-ago African snail. The gardener is the pupil; it is the garden that teaches.

Miyano has created his tropical paradise using plants that are native or appropriate to his plot. And though he now works as a garden designer in various parts of Hawaii and finds that making gardens for other people is both interesting and challenging, it is to his own tropical acre that he returns, to enclose himself in a world of green.

CURTAIN OF GREEN
Miyano and his wife, Karen, rest on their lanai, surrounded by bells, driftwood, lanterns, and varied shades and textures of green. Thriving in the rich local soil and tropical climate, plants form a curtain around the house and often grow larger than average.

JAPAN
and china

In the first half of the 17th century, Japan, angered by the interference of the Christian Church and other foreign influences, expelled all non-Japanese, save for a single Dutch factory, whose occupants were squeezed onto a tiny man-made island of Nagasaki. "Think no more of us," the Japanese said to a group of Portuguese envoys, "just as if we were no longer in the world." ∎ For 200 years Japan was the bump under the blanket. Westerners, drawn by the riches this deliciously hidden land might conceal, poked and prodded to no avail. When the blanket was finally pulled back in 1854, it was because U.S. Commodore Matthew Perry arrived in Uraga harbor with an unanswerable argument in favor of civilized concourse: ten heavily armed ships. The gunboats left and foreigners once again had access to the islands, where one of the things that caught their eye was the Japanese garden. Though its origin lay back in the seventh century, when an envoy returned from China and created his own version of the Chinese emperor's pleasure park, the copies had long since surpassed the original. ∎ The gardens of Japan are subtler than their precedents. The Chinese garden, with its lacquered bridges and buildings with swooping roofs, is a statement. The Japanese garden is a hint that leads the viewer to finish the thought. But in both countries the garden is created as a place of peace, where opposites are put into balance: the height of the mountain anchoring the depth of the sea, the lightness and motion of sand raked into curves flowing past the weight and stillness of a stone. ∎ Lafcadio Hearn, an American journalist who moved to Japan in 1890, gives an idea of the impact that these naturalistic landscapes had on the Western eye: "There are miniature hills, with old trees upon them; and there are long slopes of green, shadowed by flowering shrubs, like riverbanks; and there are green knolls like islets. All these verdant

elevations rise from spaces of pale yellow sand, smooth as a surface of silk and limiting the curves and meanderings of a river course. These sanded spaces are not to be trodden upon; they are much too beautiful for that . . . they are traversed in various directions by lines of flat unhewn rock slabs, placed at slightly irregular distances from one another, exactly like stepping-stones across a brook. The whole effect is that of the shores of a still stream in some lovely, lonesome, drowsy place." The garden was, he said, "at once a picture and a poem." ■ An idealized landscape rather than a showcase for flowers, the Japanese garden is meant to imitate nature, not defy it. Its perfection comes from a careful study of the way things are shaped and how they are placed. The gardener may train a tree into a certain form by propping its branches with poles or weighing them down with stones, but the viewer sees a pine that looks as if it has been shaped by wind and weather. Because the balance between objects is an important part of the garden, what is left out of a design is given as much thought as what is put in. The distance between objects provides both balance and boundary. And it serves another role as well: When a space is left empty, it draws the viewer in to contemplate the garden's completion. ■ In a society where ancient practices are held in high regard, it is not surprising that the Japanese garden is layered with things from the past. The Japanese religion of Shinto, as well as Buddhism and Taoism, teaches that spirits live in the natural world and that each tree, each plant, each stone contains not only its own spirit but also the spirit of its kind. A maple is a forest, a rock becomes a mountain, a sweep of perfectly placed pebbles is a stream, and sand, swept into a pattern of waves, is the sea. ■ In Japan, the gardener acknowledges that nature is the old master, and the gardener is content to copy

elements of **japanese** garden style

shakkei The concept of "borrowed view," in which elements of the surrounding scenery—such as mountains in the distance—are framed by walls, trees, or other elements and integrated into the garden's design to direct the view and expand the feeling of available space.

kare-sansui A "dry landscape" garden. First developed during the Muromachi period (1393–1558) as part of the Zen temple garden, the kare-sansui replaces trees, plants, and water with an artful arrangement of rocks and patterns raked in the sand.

karedaki A "dry waterfall," created by arranging stones, sometimes with striations or indentations that resemble water patterns. It often appears in a kare-sansui but may also be set at the edge of a pond.

tsuboniwa A small garden, originally created in an area of one *tsubo* (approximately 36 square feet), usually found in a courtyard and meant to be viewed from indoors. The small scale of the tsuboniwa is often accentuated by the placement of bonsai.

roji Technically, a "dewy path" that leads through an enclosed area to a house where the formal tea ceremony is held. Stepping-stones along the path keep the feet clean and are spaced to encourage a slow, meditative pace. The tea garden is restrained, shunning broad vistas and borrowed views, turning the mind inward in preparation for the ritual service of tea.

kaiyushiki teien A stroll garden, developed during the Edo period (1615–1867), where a path, often following the shore of a body of water, is laid out to reveal the garden slowly in a series of perfectly controlled vignettes. The stroll garden utilizes the techniques of shakkei and the hide-and-reveal landscape.

tsukubai An arrangement of stones in a tea garden, including a water basin—known as a *chozubachi*—used for the ritual cleansing of hands and mouth before the tea ceremony, and a stone to hold a *toro*, or lantern. (Tsukubai also sometimes refers to a low-set water basin.) The photo opposite shows a chozubachi in the Hotel Passtel garden in Kyoto.

a world in symbols

The Shintoists believe that divine spirits live in nature, residing in a tree, a mountain, or a single stone. Taoism teaches that men and women who have achieved perfect harmony live together on five faraway islands, where they are served by sea turtles and cranes. Buddhists contemplate the natural world as an aid to meditation, which is the path to nirvana.

Nature and what nature symbolizes are inextricably intertwined in the Eastern garden, where trees, stones, islands, and water have meanings that are not immediately apparent to the Western eye. A visitor who does not know what lies behind the elements of the garden can certainly enjoy its beauty, but to be soothed by a song's melody is not as satisfying if you do not understand the words that give it meaning.

A miniature mountain shaped of gravel or earth is not just a design element; it represents the Hindu-Buddhist belief that a mountain stands at the center of the world. Ascending the slope is a metaphor for reaching enlightenment. The evergreen pine, which holds its needles when other trees drop their leaves, is a symbol of permanence. The straight stalks and uniform growth of bamboo are seen as expressions of strength and reliability. Because the blossoms of the plum tree may open during spring snows, they symbolize rebirth; and because the flowers fall before they wither, they are signs of longevity. In Chinese gardens, the peony symbolizes happiness; in the Japanese garden, the camellia holds that distinction.

Enjoyment of the Eastern garden comes from the physical perfection of its parts, but also from the serenity that lies in contemplating the spiritual meaning within it.

BAMBOO GROVE, PEBBLE STREAM Bamboo (above) holds an important place in the Japanese garden, planted as much for the symbolism of its strength as for the sound of the wind rustling through the grove. Opposite: Smooth river stones in a dry "stream" at Shinnyo-in in Kyoto are arranged in a fish-scale pattern to imitate the fluidity of water.

TINY WORLDS

At the Suizen-ji garden in Kumamoto (this page), the volcanic cone of Mount Fuji is rendered in miniature. *Tsukiyama*, or "artificial hills," were common features in 17th-century stroll gardens. Opposite: The Japanese skill at extracting the essence of nature reaches its peak in bonsai, a form of miniaturization that became popular during the Edo period. Unable to emulate royal gardens, with their large tracts of land, merchants embraced the art of dwarfing and shaping trees in earthenware pots: a forest contained in a single tree.

271

the shaping of nature

For more than a thousand years, the Japanese have been paying tribute to nature in gardens where a mountain is condensed into a single stone and an ocean lies in a tiny pool. "Recalling one's memories of wild nature . . . reflecting on nature again and again" was how the mid-11th-century gardening book *Sakuteiki* described the experience of being in a garden. But the westerner finds a paradox: This reverence for the natural is expressed in highly unnatural ways. Instead of letting time and weather shape the world, the Japanese gardener makes nature do what it's told. Stones, with their hard certainty, are arranged to imitate the liquid flow of a river, moss becomes a greensward, and soft, slippery sand holds patterns no beach has ever seen.

Is a pine tree failing to droop in the desired fashion? Then small rocks, bound up like parcels, will be tied to its branches to pull them into the favored form and bamboo and twine will be used to encourage them to swoop gracefully rather than stand stiffly upright. Like a child with a mouthful of metal, the tree will need several years in its binding before it settles down and accepts its altered appearance. Forever after the trunk will have a curve—the kind of look an ancient tree gets from years of growing on the edge of a cliff in the face of enduring gales. This "character pine" will then draw the eye toward beautiful spots in the garden.

This delight in the shape of things is evident in the choice of a standing stone or the curve of a path. For the westerner this is another paradox: In its gardens, a nation that favors conformity in almost everything else reserves its highest honor for that which is unique.

FORMAL TRAINING
To preserve the shape of a sand cone at Ginkaku-ji in Kyoto (above), gardeners smooth the surface using wooden mason's trowels. Opposite: A pine tree at Koishikawa Korakuen in Tokyo has been bound and trained to look like it was shaped by natural forces. Japanese gardeners say that binding a tree not only encourages strong, graceful growth but also protects against insect infestation.

WINTERBOUND

Japanese gardeners, accustomed to wrapping, pruning, and tying their trees for shape and beauty, may also go to extraordinary lengths to protect their treasured plants from the elements. In the gardens of Katsura Villa, the Imperial Palace in Kyoto, workers bind cycads with straw to shield them from the harshness of winter. Rice-fiber ropes may also be used to protect pine branches from breaking under the weight of snow.

the master
gadener

In Japan, *sensei* is the word for "teacher," the mentor who guides apprentices through the intricacies of their discipline, be it *ikebana* (flower arrangement), *cha-no-yu* (the tea ceremony), or *kabuki* theater. When the students are ready, the sensei, like good teachers everywhere, lets them go.

Julie Moir Messervy, a landscape designer and author of *The Inward Garden*, had just such a sensei when she studied garden making in Japan.

His name was Kinsaku Nakane, and though he died several years ago, he stands as a symbol of those who preserved and passed along the art and craft of making a Japanese garden. When placing a stone in a landscape, Messervy recalls, "he would motion for me to stand behind him and then, without a word, would direct his men to dig the rock into the ground, tilt it, turn it so that it stood exactly right, both alone and in relation to everything around it."

After graduating from university, Nakane apprenticed himself to a Kyoto gardener for three years, learning about maintenance and construction— weeding and sweeping, pruning and fence building, positioning rocks and trees as a member of a crew restoring ancient landscapes. One of his finest designs was his very first, a garden at Kyoto's Jonangu shrine, built in 1954, when he was just 38.

During the next four decades, as he constructed hundreds of parks and gardens in Japan and around the world, Nakane shared his wisdom with students, both Japanese and foreign. His aim was simple: to help others appreciate the Japanese garden as a model for how landscapes and human society should interrelate. "If someone stops to see the tree I planted by a stream," he said, "which has grown well and casts its lovely shadow on the water—and he feels that it is beautiful—his mind has drawn closer to my world of beauty. Herein lies the delight of a designer."

SENSEI'S LESSONS
The late garden master Kinsaku Nakane (opposite top) advised his apprentices to learn and honor the traditions of the Japanese garden but not to be bound by convention. Nakane studied the moss garden (this page) at Saihō-ji in Kyoto for a full year before starting his own design practice. Among the many projects he worked on during his career was the renovation of the garden at Daisen-in in Kyoto (opposite bottom), where rocks and gravel are used to create a dry river and waterfall—a *karedaki*.

277

the art of stone

With a perception many westerners of his generation were unable to share, the American journalist Lafcadio Hearn wrote: "In order to comprehend the beauty of a Japanese garden, it is necessary to understand . . . the beauty of stones. Not of stones quarried by the hand of man, but of stones shaped by nature only. Until you can feel, and keenly feel, that stones have character, that stones have tones and values, the whole artistic meaning of a Japanese garden cannot be revealed to you."

To make a Japanese garden, you must ask a stone where it would like to be. "In the work of stone arrangement, you should first complete the placing of the principal stone having a distinct character, and then proceed to set other stones complying with the 'requesting' mood of the principal stone," advises the *Sakuteiki*. A stone set in a stream will be shifted dozens of times until it looks as though it has forced its way up through the earth to divide the freshets of water flowing around it.

At one time stones were thought to contain divine powers, a life force that could influence the fortunes of the people who lived near them. Stones of the right color, the right shape, set in harmonious balance, would bring a family good luck. Properly placed, they helped to keep good energy flowing in a household. Improperly placed, they could throw things out of balance and bring disaster.

Even the stepping-stones on the path of a stroll garden are set with a purpose: to slow the pace, not—as would be the Western way—to provide footholds to race from start to finish. In a Japanese garden, to rush is to lose the time one needs to meditate on its meaning.

LIGHT AND SAND
Toro, or "lanterns" (above), were originally used to illuminate the front of Buddhist temples; today they often serve as sculptural elements in the garden. Opposite: In the 20th-century *kare-sansui* ("dry landscape" garden) at Tofuku-ji in Kyoto, "mountain islands" in the form of rocks emerge from a "sea" of undulating raked granite gravel.

PATHS OF GLORY
Stones of various shapes,
and sizes (this page) have
been artfully laid to create
a path at Koetsu-ji in
Kyoto. Opposite: Ferns
grow up through a naturalistic ground cover of
stones, large and small. In
the Japanese garden, paths
are consciously designed
to convey a mood—from
formal to informal—and
control how the space is
experienced. If the stones
are uneven, the visitor is
forced to focus on the
path itself, whereas flat
or evenly laid stones allow
the visitor to focus on
views of the garden.

a tranquil enclosure

Hidden behind bamboo screens or enclosing walls, the *tsuboniwa*, the small courtyard garden, is named after the *tsubo*, a measurement of approximately 36 square feet. Though it may be larger than a single tsubo, this tiny garden is meant to be viewed from indoors.

If the Japanese garden is a re-creation of nature, the tsuboniwa is its reduction, providing a small-scale, private window on the natural world. Like a miniature stage set, the tsuboniwa is often laid out to be viewed from a single vantage point. Unlike the American balcony or patio garden, it is for looking at, not for sitting in.

The tsuboniwa may be the ultimate example of reduction in the Japanese garden, but there are other types of gardens that shut out the world. The *roji*, or tea garden, is designed to turn the mind inward, to prepare for the ceremony of tea. Planted along a single path, with stepping-stones placed to slow the feet, its purpose is to shut away the outside world, to let the mind float free.

The *kare-sansui*, the epitome of the Zen landscape, is further enclosed, further refined—a garden in essence only, usually containing only sand and stone, arranged with the utmost attention to balance and placement. These contemplative gardens of the Zen monks are places of quiet and incredible beauty. Stare long enough and the rippling patterns of sand turn into a sea, a simple stone grows into an island. Stare longer still, and island and sea disappear into the eternal void.

The wisdom of the Japanese is in knowing that to enclose is not to confine, but to create boundaries that encourage contemplation.

INWARD FOCUS
A roofed gate frames a view of Saiho-ji in Kyoto (above), whose grounds were landscaped as an earthly version of Buddhist paradise. Opposite: The tea garden is always an enclosed space, set apart from the outside world. At Sanzen-in in Kyoto, a ladle lies across the *chozubachi*, or water basin, where guests cleanse their hands and mouth before the tea ceremony.

SERENE STAGE

By enclosing a garden, the designer creates a stage set that limits and defines the space and helps it to be framed and viewed from the appropriate angle. Though Ritsurin-en in Takamatsu encompasses an enormous stroll garden, the teahouse garden is an intimate, contained space, shaped by translucent walls, sliding doors, and posts framing a wide veranda. The placement of a stone water basin, twisted pines, and raked gravel gives the area a feeling of meditative serenity.

bringing it
HOME

As more Americans move to cities and suburbs, and open spaces disappear, gardeners have begun to look at the way the gardens of the East are able to bring nature into the smallest places. Although a Japanese stroll garden can cover acres, it can also be adapted to a suburban lot, where a wandering path revealing hidden views makes the space seem larger. The smallest balcony can become a *tsuboniwa*, a meditative garden to be viewed from within. An urban backyard, placed between towering buildings that block out the sun, can hold the raked sand and symbolic stones of a *kare-sansui*. The concept of *shakkei*, or "borrowed view," lets the gardener take advantage of the landscape beyond or use a moon gate to frame a neighboring tree. The most important thing Americans have learned from the Japanese is to seek the essence of nature—in a bed of moss under a shady tree or in the miniature world of a bonsai pot—and to appreciate the art of small things.

Stone River

Water is an important element in the Eastern garden, and when it is unavailable, sand, gravel, or stones may be arranged in patterns to symbolize its motion. The dry stream here—created for an exhibition at the Enid A. Haupt Conservatory at the New York Botanical Garden in the Bronx—rises out of a clump of flowers, flows under a bamboo bridge, and disappears into a stand of bamboo. The effect is created by excavating a bed to a depth of 6–10 inches and pitching it on a gradual slant so rainwater will run off and not turn the bed into a bog. The bottom is covered with 3–6 inches of gravel, then two or three layers of stones are laid on top. The stones in the final layer must be similar in size and shape, pointing in the same direction and overlapping like fish scales. Laying the stones in swirls suggests eddies or pools. A dry pebble stream looks most convincing when, like this one, it flows toward a low spot in the terrain, wanders through the landscape, then trickles out of sight.

287

East in the West

Nobuo Matsunaga, formerly Japan's ambassador to the United States, called the Japanese Garden of Portland, Oregon, "the most beautiful Japanese garden outside of Japan." The authenticity of the garden, designed in 1963 by the late Takuma Tono, a professor and garden designer based in Sapporo, Japan, remains unquestioned. The Sand and Stone Garden (right), surrounded by a wall capped with Gifu tiles, uses raked sand in the manner of Ryoan-ji in Kyoto, one of the best examples of the classical Zen garden. In the dry garden, the patterns, which are raked into the sand with a special tool, are symbolic of water. In Portland's Strolling Pond Garden (left), stones are artfully placed in a stream lined with maples and punctuated by a stone *toro*, or "lantern," on one bank. Toro, originally used to illuminate the fronts of Buddhist temples, represent the triumph of light over darkness.

Falling Water

Osamu and Holly Shimizu have created an idyllic sanctuary in their 30-by-50-foot backyard outside Washington, D.C. A narrow, 6-foot-long stream runs down a man-made mound, becoming a waterfall that tumbles over a flagstone shelf and cascades past trailing variegated ivy into a 16-by-26-foot pool. The waterfall garden, Holly Shimizu says, "was designed to make the most of water's wide range and deep versatility. The timbre varies as water moves over and around the rocks at different levels along its path." To build their sloping water garden, the Shimizus began at the bottom and worked their way up. After determining that the stream and waterfall required an elevation of 4 to 6 feet, they piled up a mound of gravel and rock (old brick and concrete chunks would work well, too), and covered it with soil from the pool excavation.

The stream (1) began with a 2- to 3-inch-deep base of sand covered with a rubber pool liner. A 2-inch-deep layer of cement was poured over the liner and a 3- to 5-inch layer of stones was set into it. The waterfall (2) was built from flat stones mortared together and supported by the cinder-block wall of the pool and a base of concrete over gravel. The pool pump (3) pushes the water 70 feet through a small pipe to the top of the stream.

Strolling Stones Gather Moss

Moss gardens, green and spongy underfoot, have been planted in traditional Eastern gardens for many years. They are found particularly in deeply shaded areas, since moss thrives where other plants cannot, reproducing by throwing out billions of spores. Because it softens the outlines of man-made objects and binds them to the natural setting, moss is also encouraged to grow around stone water basins, lanterns, or sculptures. In a private garden in Memphis, Tennessee (right), moss grows between paving stones, turning a curved path into a serene green mosaic. To preserve the look of a soft green carpet, pull weeds or sprouting tree seedlings in early summer; remove falling leaves quickly in autumn before they smother the moss. To encourage moss to spread, test the soil; moss prefers soil that is slightly acidic (5–5.5 pH).

Pruned and Potted

The ultimate enclosed garden is the bonsai pot, and the miniaturized plants have needs as specific as those of their full-size relatives. Bonsai fail, says Robert Mahler, curator of bonsai at the Brooklyn Botanic Garden, when temperate-zone species such as evergreens are grown in the house, in temperatures too high to bring on dormancy. Mahler's suggestions for bonsai that will grow well indoors: *Carissa grandiflora*, Natal plum (left), with fragrant white flowers that appear on and off all year (a variegated form stands next to the pruning shears and wires that are used for shaping the plant, bottom right); *Serissa foetida*, with pink or white flowers that blossom at intervals throughout the year; *Punica granatum* 'Nana', a pomegranate with vermillion blossoms; and white-flowering *Syzygium paniculatum*, brush cherry (with its trained trunk, top right).

Flat-out Simplicity

In a serene landscape designed by Douglas Reed for art dealer Ellen Kern, stones laid both vertically and horizontally make patterns in the grass (left). Reed separated the bluestone treads and risers so that the lawn flows through the steps, calling attention not only to the natural simplicity of the stones but also to the gentle slope of the land. In his designs Reed tries to express the essence of the natural landscape; he cites among his influences the 800-year-old moss garden at Saiho-ji in Kyoto.

Directing the Eye

On a tiny Seattle lot, designer Dan Borroff has incorporated the Eastern design principles of creating miniaturized space and, as he says, "experimenting with perception through symbolic effects." In the back garden (right), only 17 feet wide, diagonal brick lines cut across the slate paving, serving as arrows to direct the eye; a basalt boulder framed by the grassy forms of cytisus, stipa, and miscanthus draws attention downward from the enclosing fence.

297

STONE: PLACEMENT

Healing Stones

Like stones in a Japanese garden, the boulders in the 7-acre National AIDS Memorial Grove in San Francisco help create a contemplative space. At the grove's eastern edge (left), the Circle of Friends bears the names of donors. Indentations in the boulders accept flowers and remembrances, and visitors make surreptitious "donations" of plants and seeds. "I'm not sure I ever want it to be finished," says one of the grove's designers, Michael Boland. "The power of this place comes from the opportunities for healing through action."

Now and Zen

Richard Cohen and Jim Kutz, partners in the landscape firm Rockwater in Amagansett, New York, used boulders at the edge of a "lake" of raked sand with clumps of juniper representing a forest (right). Instead of imposing on the land, the designers allow the land to instruct them. "There must be rhythm in the way rocks are placed, but nothing's regular or symmetrical," says Kutz. "We'll put a rock down, walk away, look at it, then go back and move it again."

Liquid Assets

When nursery owners Paul and Mardell Steinkamp of Altamont, New York, decided to create a water feature in the enclosure between their residence and their nursery, they built an entire series of pools. A concrete trough surmounted by variegated grasses (top left) spills water into a reflecting pool, which is separated by a wooden bridge from a planted water garden. The pool in the foreground (bottom left) is edged with hostas; the bogs in the background hold calla lilies, fountain grass, sedges, cannas, and *Eupatorium* 'Gateway'. Yellow groove bamboo (right) graces the view of pools, bogs, bridge, and trough.

302

Framed View

"Every now and then," says Ralph Ammirati, a partner at a Manhattan ad agency, "I turn my head away from my office and look out the window. Just inches from me is this calming, serene, beautiful Japanese garden." The garden (left) was built by landscape designer Jeff Mendoza on an 18-by-32-foot rooftop. Inside the frame—made of galvanized steel, Mexican river stones, and a band of *Sedum sexangulare*—is a field of fine, small Japanese stones. A planter filled with *Miscanthus sinensis* 'Gracillimus' is set off-center for asymmetry.

Tree of Tranquillity

A staple of the Eastern garden, the Japanese red maple (*Acer palmatum* 'Atropurpureum'), lends its elegant structure, delicately shaped leaves, and brilliant color to a 14-by-16-foot courtyard (right) in Washington, D.C. Garden designer Jane MacLeish made the tree the centerpiece of the enclosed garden, but she pruned it to keep it from being an overpowering presence. "For me," she explains, "small spaces should be quiet spaces."

Windows onto a Secluded World

A new Chinese scholar's garden at the Staten Island Botanical Garden—the first such garden built on American soil—demonstrates the importance of architecture in shaping the view in an Eastern garden. Opened in 1999, the garden was a collaboration between the Landscape Architecture Corporation of China and Demetri Sarantitis Architects in Manhattan. The peaceful garden with its enclosed spaces is named for the scholar gentry who, after the Mongol invasion of China in the 13th century, shunned the new capital in Beijing and retreated into the secluded world of painting and gardening, "shrinking the earth to contain the vastness." A "leaky window" in the scholar's garden (left)— a fanciful grillwork opening in a geometric or floral design—draws the eye to what lies on the other side. Another common aperture, the moon gate (right), is a circular portal that both frames the vista beyond and provides access to it.

garden
TOUR

When you have a clear understanding of a Japanese garden, you have a clear understanding of the Japanese culture," says Pierre Sernet, an Internet executive who has created a rooftop tea garden on Manhattan's Upper East Side. "The Shinto religion has tremendous respect for nature. The gardens are supposed to be a representation of nature."

Four floors below, Manhattan is carrying on its cacophonous symphony, but here there is only the splash of water and the song of birds. Watching the avian population from the *engawa*, a wooden platform that stands outside his bedroom door, Sernet surveys a garden that has slipped the bonds of place and time. It could be Kyoto a hundred years ago; somewhere out of sight a kimono-clad figure could be bending to light charcoal to make tea.

The green leaves of bamboo droop over the *tsukubai*, a stone basin filled with water splashing from a hollow bamboo pipe. The basin *(continued on page 310)*

INSIDE VIEW
A view from the teahouse shows the engawa (platform) leading to the apartment. In the foreground is a Japanese black pine that Sernet has trained to its current shape. In the background is the tsukubai, or water basin, used for purifying the mouth and hands before the tea ceremony.

Rooftop Retreat

When seen from above (opposite top), Sernet's Japanese garden looks like any other rooftop garden in New York City. Only when the visitor is inside the concealing foliage does it become clear that Sernet has adapted the centuries-old traditions of Japanese gardeners. In the front of the garden (opposite bottom), a bamboo spout sends water into the tsukubai, made of lava rock to minimize weight on the roof. A gate flanked by azaleas (left) separates the front of the garden from the back, where the teahouse resides. Black cord has been used to tie the bamboo pieces together.

Garden Plan

1. Roof of engawa
2. Tsukubai
3. Stairway to upper roof
4. California redwood
5. Hemlock
6. Skylight
7. Stepping-stones
8. Japanese black pine
9. Azaleas
10. Teahouse
11. Weeping cherry
12. Shade tree (mimosa)

(continued from page 306) is surrounded by smooth black stones representing the sea. Very mystical. A stone stands ready to hold a lantern—or in 20th-century New York, a parcel or purse. Very practical.

The path to the teahouse curves past a Japanese maple and azaleas shaped into cushiony mounds, past Japanese barberry (*Berberis thunbergii* 'Atropurpurea') and low-growing Japanese junipers (*Juniperus procumbens* 'Nana.'). A Japanese black pine droops artistically. "I have tortured this one a lot," says Sernet, affectionately patting the tree, which is bound down with stones to twist it into the desired shape. Atlas cedars (*Cedrus libani* subsp. *atlantica*) and a California redwood (*Sequoia sempervirens*) stand sentinel as the path disappears through a bamboo gate set in a bamboo fence. The area where the tea ceremony is held is secluded, shut off from the world.

Like any illusion, creating an Eastern garden on a Western site only 42 feet long by 20 feet wide is one part trick and nine parts work. Here the principal trick is one of perspective. The garden is divided so that two-thirds is visible and the view of the remainder is obstructed. To increase the visual effect, Sernet used large-leaved plants in the foreground and smaller-leaved ones farther away. The stones in the path also decrease in size as they move through the garden.

All illusions need something to rest on, and a New York roof is a fragile support. Before bringing in a single plant, Sernet fiberglassed the roof to keep it from leaking. In laying out the garden, he took care that each heavy tree was positioned on top of a supporting beam, evenly distributing the weight.

A computerized watering system that "pops up, sprays out, and goes down" keeps the garden from drying out. "In the city, you have tremendous heat and evaporation. If you don't have constant moisture," he says, "your garden is gone."

To minimize the weight of the tsukubai, Sernet carved it out of light lava rock. The trees and plants grow in low, tin-lined, modular plywood boxes and are fed manure and fertilizer. He also regularly tests the soil to make sure the plants are getting the nutrients they need.

Sernet has used one other trick. He has enlisted the help of four ancient stone Buddhas, whose judicious placement undoubtedly helps to keep the garden green.

NATURE ENCLOSED
The engawa opens onto a path of stepping-stones, which lead the eye toward the teahouse, although the full path is not revealed. Azaleas clipped in mounds face Japanese barberry (*Berberis thunbergii* 'Atropurpurea') across the path. In the foreground is a *Pieris japonica* and a towering California redwood (*Sequoia sempervirens*).

SHAPE DU JOUR
France's passion for gardening—and geometry—crops up at L'Art du Jardin, a spring garden festival where fashion-conscious Parisians snatch up the latest in plant trends, such as these ornamental orbs of baby boxwood plants.

index

*Page references in **boldface** indicate photographs or illustrations.*

GREEN ROOMS
On the grounds of the
American Academy in
Rome, boxwood hedges
rim a fountain, creating a
place to pause and muse
on the view. Beyond is
green architecture—a
backdrop of pleached
Quercus ilex.

credits

KEY: T = top, B = bottom, L = left
C = center, R = right

Cover . . . . a field of *Tulipa greigii* 'Cape Cod',
at Keukenhof in Lisse, Netherlands
by Ron van Dongen
Page 2 . . . . grounds of the American
Academy in Rome by Maura McEvoy
Pages 6–7 . . . . Susan Seubert

CHAPTER 1

CHAPTER 2

CHAPTER 3

CHAPTER 4

CHAPTER 5

CHAPTER 6